A JOURNAL
FROM THE INSIDE

BY
Ray Rivers

Copyright © 2025 by Ray Rivers

All Rights Reserved. No part of this publication may be reproduced, stored in a retrieval system, or transmitted, in any form or by any means, electronic, mechanical, photocopying, recording, or otherwise, without the written permission of the author.

Published by : USA Publishing Hub
Printed In United States of America

Contents

Chapter One 1

Chapter Two 26

Chapter Three 49

Chapter Four 63

Chapter Five 77

Chapter Six 91

Chapter Seven 105

Chapter Eight 133

Chapter Nine 143

Chapter Ten 161

Chapter Eleven 183

Chapter Twelve 220

Chapter Thirteen 239

Chapter Fourteen 269

Chapter Fifteen 285

Chapter One

The sun screamed heated rays through the front windshield while we sat sweating in the blazer, contemplating whether we were ready to go through with the robbery.

We had been through this routine several times; this time…was different. It was broad daylight and kids were being dropped off at the bus stop across the street from us. We were in unfamiliar territory reputedly hostile for blacks. The stench of nervousness shrouded the truck as our adrenaline peaked.

"What's up? We doing this or what? I know the money in there is stacked because they never do drops. Somebody on the inside told me how much bread be in that place at one time. One minute from now and we paid."

Hedrick was making it sound so simple.

Dre and I bit at the bait for fast, easy money.

Moments earlier, we were all headed to the mall to shop, but made an unscheduled stop to get some extra cash. We landed outside this store located in the hellish part of the country.

The Wild West was a better term for the gun toting, constitutional upholders. They believed in the right to bear arms and the right to fire them practically at will. They were close and they were the law despite not brandishing a badge to authorize them as lawmen—which made our pit stop even more psychotic. We were just as dangerous, only we were out of our urban sprawl, the very element that sanctioned our actions.

The robbery seemed foolproof…

The thought of easy money was just as convincing. We were parked about a quarter of a mile away from the store at a boat dock. From our vantage point, we cased the store to foolproof our plans. At first glance, the store looked to be dejected. There was a gas pump with four nozzles in front of the store. The building was small with dirt-stained windows and covered in faded old advertising decals.

The store was in the middle of a small-town square which had a family-owned restaurant to the left side of it, a neighborhood in back, and a small mechanic shop to the right. About three cars and four huge trucks were parked at the restaurant from what I could see and the mechanic shop looked to be closed for the day. From a distance, the store appeared to be simple enough to rob.

We made our move without fear.

This was not our first foray.

We were craftsmen in this trade and highly successful up until this point. I double checked my tech-nine to ensure it was fire ready just in case our plans got upended. Hedrick popped open the glove compartment and pulled out his thirty-eight specials. Dre was to be the get-away driver while we handled the brunt of the work.

An all too familiar shiver danced the length of my spine. (Pre-game jitters)

We drove to the front door. Hedrick and I jumped out in full stride. Mercenaries prepped for war. Hedrick ran in while I dashed to the corner of the store, alertly watchful of the restaurant and parking lot. Not quite forty-five seconds later, a rusted brown pick-up truck with huge tires, a cracked windshield, and clay-colored grime layered along the sides of it, pulled into the store lot.

It did not take a rocket scientist to assess the situation. The red-neck driving the truck made a beeline to the restaurant. As he sped past me, I caught a glimpse of a rifle – in a rack – in the rear window.

I bolted inside the store. The bell on the door chimed vibrantly from my forceful entrance. Hedrick was pointing the pistol at a balding white male sprawled face down on the floor. He was stuffing wads of bills into a brown paper bag with his free hand.

"Hey man, it's time to bounce. Looks like they about to get a war party across the street. Some fool done peeped out what's going down in here and he strapped."

Hedrick's eyes bulged like a fiend with fear. We had been on many robberies but rarely ended in a shoot-out.

I could tell he was scared. He ran past me with the money bag and looked out the door. When he turned around his mouth was open for flies.

"Man, it's three dudes with guns running over here."

His voice was cracked with fear. Our plans had turned to shit. And so did our strategy.

He ran out the door before I could catch up to him. He did not give a damn whether I got shot in the back by the same guy he had just robbed.

My mind was racing a million thoughts a second. Either run out shooting or take a risk getting gunned down trying to make it to the truck. Just as I was about to exit…the worst thing to ever happen in a robbery happened.

Dre jumped out of the truck and screamed to Hedrick to turn around. The car had shut down and would not start. We later found out that in a panic, Dre had cut the truck off while it was still in drive by accident when he saw the guys with the guns. He never realized the car was still in drive when he tried to crank it back up.

Yeah, it was dumb but fear makes one do irrational shit when facing death.

Hedrick handed Dre the large bag of money and kept running toward his truck. I assumed he knew some trick to get it back rolling. Time was running out fast. He dove in the front seat. Seconds later, the sound of the engine was music to my ears. I burst through the door and ran toward the truck. Rapid gunfire erupted to the right of me. I glanced in the direction of the vigilantes while in full stride. One of them was squatted on one knee, firing rounds as if he were a military sniper taking out suicide bombers.

I turned on a dime, ducking unseen bullets while taking cover on the side of the store. Dre ran toward me with the most frightened look I had ever seen. The sight of Jesus could not have elicited that expression.

Hedrick stomped the gas pedal to the floor. Smoke streamed from the tires as he burnt rubber fleeing the scene. I could not believe it. My best friend of fifteen years was leaving me to die. My heart sank in the bowels of my stomach. The men turned toward us and began advancing with rifles drawn. They were in sync like an elite military unit. This was their territory- Vietnam familiarity and I was the invader.

Dre screamed in panic mode.

"How he gone leave us like this. Man, this shit fucked up. We bout to get killed out here in the country."

I was a survivor. Always the leader who focused on solutions rather than the problem.

"Shut up and follow me," I whispered.

We scooted along the edge of the store until we reached the opposite end from our assailants then rounded the corner. Not quite thirty feet ahead of us, a short, skinny white guy was crouching low to the ground. They were trying to corner us in like herded cattle for a slaughter.

Surprised at being caught at his clandestine operation, he ducked behind an old boat that looked to be older than a fossil.

His fear gave us an opening. We hauled ass in the direction of the neighborhood. The only thing separating us from victory was a rickety wooden fence that I was about to scale in one leap. I was a four-time state track runner and an ex- football jock. Dre could not match my speed.

I was ahead of Dre when I heard the loud pop of gunfire boom six or seven times in repetition. The rapid fire could easily have passed for fully automatic gunfire to the untrained ear. I leaned forward and turned on the speed at the sound of the gunfire. Something was not right. I no longer heard the steady drum of Dre's shoes pounding the loose gravel behind me.

Instinctively, I turned around just in time to see Dre lying on the ground writhing in pain. Blood was flowing from both of his legs. Just beyond Dre, the shooter was squatted on one knee, re-loading with blazing speed.

Perspiration broke out all over me. My heart beat the inside of my chest like a victim held hostage in a trunk. I had to make a hurried decision whether to save Dre or abandon him the way Hedrick did. I was born into code. The streets had battle hardened rules of engagement like the military. Never leave a comrade behind. I ran toward him. He was yelling something about his legs but I could not hear him throughout all the commotion. Soon as I reached him the shooter stood up and took aim for the kill shot.

This moment had come down to a duel and I was much faster. I raised the tech nine and fired rounds sporadically in his direction. He ducked back out of sight. Desperate now for survival, I lifted Dre off the ground and wrapped his arm around my neck in one fluid motion. He screamed in pain as we hobbled together the rest of the distance to the neighborhood.

A rickety wooden fence long passed repair was the only obstacle standing in our way to safety amongst the neighborhood. I kicked several boards loose and shoved Dre under the fence.

Despite being shot, he was still clutching the money bag in a death grip. I focused my gaze on his legs. He was in bad shape, leaving us no option for a getaway on foot. His pants legs were bedraggled with a flowing mass of thick blood. The bullet tore clean through both of his upper thighs, tearing bone and sinewy muscle before exiting out the right leg. These guys were shooting high powered rifles aimed at killing big game. I guess in their minds we were just as prized as big horn elk.

My adrenaline was on full surge and all I could think about was survival. I set eyes on a tan colored Honda parked under a tree that I took to belong to the owners of the trailer we were leaning against. "Stay here and keep quiet," I told Dre, "I'm about to get us a ride."

I gripped the tech-nine like a life line and bolted up the wooden steps to the front door. A wary listener would have mistaken me for a police officer serving a search warrant the way I pounded on the door.

Twelve agonizing seconds ticked by.

Patience was not a virtue.

I twisted the knob and to my dismay it opened. The door swung open forcefully, slamming against the wall so hard it shook the entire foundation. A startled Mexican couple were hurriedly putting on their clothes, angry expressions lining both their faces. They were obviously pissed that their lovemaking was being interrupted by some rude punk. The man was about to say something until he noticed the tech nine gripped in my palm. The couple fell back against the couch, encircling each other as though they were bracing themselves for an incessant spatter of bullets.

A brazen wail escaped the lady's lips. There was so much fear flashing in her eyes that I almost turned around to leave. The need to survive far surpassed all empathy. I needed those car keys.

"Keys," I blurted out, "Where's the damn keys to the Honda parked outside?"

A misunderstanding look swept across the guy's face and I knew he didn't understand a word I was saying. I made a driving motion with my hands, turning an invisible steering wheel in the air for clarification.

They both pointed to a coffee table that was full of small picture frames. A set of keys attached to a metal key ring lay between them. I grabbed the keys and jetted back out the door to the Honda. The door was already unlocked. One turn of the key and the engine came to life.

Dre was still leaning against the trailer when I stopped the car in front of him. He was no longer the cocky, take-charge Dre I was used too. His eyes were locked in a dazed expression and his breathing was labored as he struggled to catch his breath. I sprinted to Dre as fast as humanly possible. He was reaching out to me before I was within arm's reach of him. I grabbed him in a sort of bear hug and fast walked him to the passenger side. His body fell limply against the seat. I rushed back to the drivers' side and gunned it before my door was fully closed.

I didn't want to arouse suspicion, so, I slowed the Honda down as I exited the trailer park. This getaway needed to be as Houdini like as possible. I could not have been more wrong. When I reached the stop sign to exit the trailer park, I noticed a small crowd gathering down by the store. This was our only way out.

It was obvious that the Mexican had called some people in the vicinity and warned them to be on the lookout for his car. Dre sat bolt upright and scanned the crowd until he spotted the guy that disabled both of his legs. Dre snapped his head in my direction with the speed of a fox. I could smell fear squeezing through his pores and his bottom lip was trembling a million vibrations a minute. "Shit man, they got us blocked the fuck in. How da hell we spose to get outta here?"

Without answering the question, I grabbed the tech nine from between the seats and hit the gas pedal, heading straight toward the crowd. I was so pissed off that I couldn't concentrate on anything but escape. Dre was screaming something about suicide but my rage was tuning him out.

Everything was going in one ear and out the other. The speedometer reached sixty in no time and the crowd started scattering as soon as they realized that slowing down was not an option for me. When I reached the stop sign to turn off the road, Dre started panicking. He was looking backwards and screaming for me to speed up.

"Hey Ray, drive faster man. Mash out cause it's a buncha dudes just got behind us in dat red truck."

I glanced in the rear view at the cloud of dust left in the wake of the acceleration of the truck. The driver was speeding madly toward us and he was gaining ground fast. I stomped the gas and hung the right turn so hard that the Honda fishtailed several times before straightening back up. The men in the truck hung the turn just as hard as I, surely intent on running us off the road. The gap was diminishing faster than a thirty-second-time bomb. We were on a two-lane road that was not very wide at all. Our only chances of survival would be in outsmarting our assailants.

The police stopped as we crossed the county line but the red truck full of armed vigilantes stayed on our tail.

The small V6 engine was no match for the bigger V8 engine in the truck.

I dropped the Honda in low gear to get all I could get out of it, but no matter what I tried, the truck kept closing the gap. The speedometer had a 120-mph readout but I could not get the needle past 115mph. I had to decrease my speed to about 70mph as a torturous curve loomed a couple hundred yards in front of me. The tires wobbled a bit before catching enough traction to straighten up the Honda and regain the original speed of 115mph.

The truck driver did not miss a beat. He rounded the curve with the rapid smoothness and control of a veteran Nascar driver. A second wrenching curve suddenly appeared before me. I had to decrease my speed well ahead of the curve because a small Toyota was snail creeping in front of me—completely oblivious to the heart pounding chase behind them.

An eighteen-wheeler was fast approaching in the left lane, which was oncoming traffic and my assailants were within thirty yards of my bumper.

Without thinking, I swerved around the Toyota, pressed the gas pedal to the floor and gained enough speed to pass it with a few precious seconds left before swerving in front of it. My assailants pulled into the oncoming traffic lane directly behind me, clearly not seeing the devious trick. I was fast pulling on their lives. I left no space between me and the Toyota. The men in the truck would either smash head on with the eighteen-wheeler or drive off the road and collide head on with one of the many pine trees lining the two-lane highway.

I could hear the raucous honking of the horn blaring from the eighteen-wheeler as the driver tried to warn them to prevent a sure fatal wreck. Dre leaned forward and gripped the dashboard, baffled and frightened that I had pulled such a stunt. The truck steered off to the left-hand side of the road, braking instantly to prevent hitting the trees.

The driver of the Toyota behind me, instantly, braked, fearful of what I would do next.

Dre had a spaced-out expression on his face, stunned at the wickedness of my actions.

I was breathing harder than a cheetah after chasing its prey and my heart pounded like bass drums in a battle of the bands show. There was no turning back now. Our best chances at escape would be to head to the next town over, ditch the car and call someone to pick us up. My plans were to get Dre to safety as soon as we were clear of the cops.

It was a brilliant plan, only it did not work because no sooner had we entered the Eufaula city limits and turned onto the four-lane highway, I passed by the E.P.D. cop cruisers that were in the oncoming traffic lane.

I tried to slow down and blend in with the regular flow of traffic but the Eufaula police had already received a call from the Henry County police. *They had my exact description.* The instant they noticed the car, the sound of squelching tires rang out like a banshee wail as the cop cars braked hard to turn around.

Smoking, burnt rubber wafted from under the tires in cloudy wisps of smoke. I heard their engines raise like they were at a dragstrip as they hastily accelerated in the traffic lane behind me.

Initially, I wanted to pull over, but once again, my irrational thinking took over.

Some idiotic thought, or maybe, it was my guilty conscience that kept telling me to drive faster and lose the police. It was a combination of adrenaline, nervousness, and the fear of going to prison for life.

Together, they created my worst enemy: *Irrational Man*.

I listened to those crazy thoughts and once again, the chase was on.

Surely, the Honda was no match for the cop cruisers but enough meandering in and out of traffic caused enough havoc that enabled me to hold a decent lead on the police. Outwitting the police was highly probable, but out smarting their radios was damn near impossible.

The cars in front of me began to fan out, giving me a clear shot at escape. I soon noticed they were fanning out because of the roadblock ahead. In the distance, police cars were scrambling trying to set up a roadblock that stretched clear across the highway.

I was approaching fast so they did not have enough time to accomplish their goal.

My speed resumed at a hundred plus miles an hour until about a hundred yards before the roadblock. I braked just enough to allow the Honda to veer to the side of the road without losing control. The Honda swerved drastically around the half-finished roadblock. Dre had reached his breaking point throughout the madness. He screamed hysterically for me to pull over so he could bail out.

"ARE YOU CRAZY, MAN?" I yelled, "They got us labeled…armed and dangerous. These muthafuckas ready right now to take us dead or alive."

Dre hollered back angrily, "Shit! My legs are hurting like hell. I need to get to a hospital really bad, man, and with yo crazy ass driving, we will be dead in a car wreck. So, pull this muthafucka over. I ain't ready to die, man."

I looked at Dre and smirked. "Ain't but one option and one option only: getting away."

Dre looked into my eyes with the most panicked expression I had ever seen on a human face.

We now had a significant lead on the police due to their unsuccessful roadblock and were fast approaching a series of dips and hills. We topped the first hill at more than a hundred MPH.

To the right side of us, was an enormous golf course with bosomy hills. A long cement embankment lined the edge of the golf course, separating it from the main highway. Dre and I were now engaged in a heated argument about what to do next. He did the most unsuspecting thing one could imagine.

I think his hysteria had driven him to insanity.

Dre jumped out of his seat as if he was dodging a hissing rattler. He grabbed the steering wheel with both hands and yanked it toward the right side of the road. I tried desperately to steer the car back toward the highway.

I over corrected badly.

The Honda veered violently toward the golf course. It skidded out of control before it collided with the cement embankment. We were airborne. The metallic chorus of crushing metal rang out like a sonic boom in my ears. I thought it was my death knell ringing me through the portals of Hell.

The Honda continued flipping in an everlasting death spiral.

Shrapnel ejected from the vehicle like a bomb blast. We were flipping at blazing speed but everything appeared to be in slow motion. Dre and I were being tossed like laundry all over the car. He was screaming to the Lord for help. I was looking for a break. The car was caving in like a tin can crushed with a giant sledge hammer. We were going to be sandwiched like a Saw movie episode if we remained in the vehicle.

Dre's prayers were loud and jumbled but still audible over the booming of crushing metal colliding with stone and hard cement. "Please, Jesus, Lord, forgive me. I don't wanna die." He screamed this over and over again. It was our best guess that he sensed this was our final moment.

It's amazing how much flashes through the mind while in the midst of death. I distinctly remember yelling "I can't die like this," before latching on to the driver side window frame and hurtling myself through the window while the Honda was in mid-air. I sailed out of the window with enough momentum to knock down a brick wall. My freedom stunt was poorly timed. The back end of the car struck me like a home-run and I felt like I was being hit out of the park.

The ground rose to meet me as I plummeted to the cement bed. My body pancake landed at an angle and I began a vicious slide across the concrete. I made several futile attempts to stop myself from sliding. The velocity burned the flesh off my fingertips, ripped away much of my clothing and continued singing every inch of exposed flesh. It felt like there was fire in my shoulders, legs, butt cheeks, and on my back. The pain was unbearable. There is a blank spot in my memory because I do not remember stopping. I'm sure I went out for a few seconds.

Some people may find this part hard to believe, but I jumped up as if nothing had ever happened. It was pure adrenaline rushing through my veins. At the moment, I did not know if I was dead or alive. In my head, I was a spirit searching for my battered corpse. I cannot explain the feeling except to say that I felt out of this world. My entire body was vibrating tremendously. I had blurred vision and my hearing was non-existent. I thought I was a wandering soul. It felt like hours had gone by but in reality, only a mere minute at the most had ticked off my biological clock.

The sound of wailing sirens echoed in my ears, snapping me out of my elusive twilight zone. My vision cleared a bit and I focused on the thick stand of trees ahead of me. I glanced briefly in the direction of the oncoming traffic. There was a line of police cars topping the small rise not quite five seconds away.

Sunlight streamed across the top of the sirens and a blinding reflection illuminated brightly in my direction. Puzzled as to what to do next, I turned around to run but a glare from a broken taillight caught my attention. I followed the trail of wreckage with a gaping stare.

Shards of broken glass, unidentifiable pieces of metal and broken headlight pieces lined the ground. My eyes rested on the tin can that used to be a Honda. The car lay mangled and crushed with the front and rear bumpers barely hanging on. The drivers' side was completely smashed in. There was no way in hell I would have survived that crash had I been strapped in a seatbelt. I was only alive because I did not freeze up.

Throughout the prevalent turmoil, I had completely forgotten about Dre whose body was trapped in the contorted tin can. A mixture of fear, adrenaline and confusion suddenly overwhelmed me. I was about to haul ass to the wreckage when the sound of car doors jarred me out of my revelry. One brief look was all it took to notice the police scattering from their cars. They were brandishing pistols and screaming at me to get on the ground.

Without hesitation, I started running in the opposite direction away from the police. or at least I thought I was about to run. I took three steps when the sound of snapping bone pulsated through my ears and my right leg collapsed from the pressure of my body weight.

There was so much adrenaline running through my veins that I never took heed to my injuries. I fell face first, smacking the ground in a splayed-out manner. Pounding footsteps were heard in the distance and I could tell the cops were swiftly approaching me. I turned over just in time to see a slightly overweight black cop hurling through the air with outstretched arms. My only reaction was to brace myself for the impact and man did it hurt like hell. The cop landed on me with the speed of a seasoned veteran whose skill could only be acquired after making hundreds of arrests.

He quickly cuffed me then tried to pull me to my feet, unbeknownst of my broken leg and cracked ribs. I let out a blood-curdling scream that jarred my tonsils and echoed through the crisp air. Stunned, the cop released his grip on my elbow and his pistol appeared in his hands as if by magic. I fell on my shoulder to ease the pressure and pain from my cracked ribs and broken leg.

I might as well had landed on my stomach.

Pain rippled through my ribcage like a thousand needles being jabbed in me at once. Two other officers hastily appeared on both sides of the black officer with vague expressions lining their chubby faces. They all looked in my direction and I could see the black officers' brow jump upwards. A grotesque frown creased his face.

"Holy shit," the fleshy jawed cop on the right yelled before stepping forward to take a closer look at my leg. I averted my gaze toward my right leg and I was not ready for what I saw. My right leg was twisted in the opposite direction. My shredded pants revealed all the bloody wounds on my leg.

The officer screaming at the top of his lungs for someone to get an ambulance was barely audible to my ears as panic and fear engulfed my entire body. Tears flooded my eyes as I lay on the hard ground, wondering dreadfully if I would ever be able to walk again. Suddenly, a spine-chilling wail resonated through my ears loud and clear like a wounded hound dog after being caught in a steel bear trap.

An officer was yelling, "OVER HERE! OVER HERE!"

He was referring to the tin can Honda. I lifted my head off the ground to see several cops running toward the wreckage. A burly officer who held what appeared to be a black crowbar broke out the back window of the Honda. Shattered glass rained all over the ground. He then crawled halfway through the car and in a matter of seconds he was scooting out backwards, dragging Dre with him.

Dre was rocking his head from, side to side and I could hear a few mumbled words about gunshots, not dying and hospitals flow dazedly from his lips. I later learned that Dre was knocked unconscious during the accident and was just beginning to wake up when his screams pierced my ears. I could only imagine the fear of waking up sandwiched between the wrecked hull of what used to be a car. I do not remember much else that happened after the officer dragged Dre from the wreck because I blacked out.

I awoke at the hospital to the sound of beeping machines and the alcoholic medicinal smell that stung my nostrils. The tips of my fingers were stinging like fire and my left shoulder felt like there was a boulder sitting on top of it. It was hard for to me to catch my breath because of my cracked ribs. Every breath felt like I was inhaling acid.

I silently prayed, hopping I was not bleeding internally. This hospital was infamous for doing a mediocre check-up and two of my friends had died from internal bleeding that was never discovered by the staff. My right hand had black stitching across four of my fingers and my right leg was propped up in a hospital wrap. There was a weeping sound at the foot of the bed so I strained my neck to see who it was.

My mother noticed I was awake and walked to my bedside looking ten years older from worry. The pain and suffering in her eyes oozed unbearable anguish. I averted my gaze to keep from meeting her gaze before she began questioning me.

"What made you do something so stupid like this, son? Whatever you needed, you should have come to me for it." I could not answer her and she sensed that I was having trouble with the question so she changed the subject briefly. She told me that Hedrick was caught at a roadblock and was being held at the county jail claiming to be innocent of all charges. We talked until the officer stepped into the room to tell my mom it was time to go. She was not ready to leave my side.

"Why do I have to leave? I'm staying here with my son so I can make sure he gets taken care of. These doctors will tell you everything is alright and the next hour, folks end up dead. I ain't leaving till I get some answers."

"Look, lady, I wasn't even supposed to let you in here," the officer growled back angrily. "He ain't a regular hospital patient. He is being detained for a criminal investigation. Two detectives have been waiting to question him about a robbery."

My mom was about to protest, but I told her I was going to be okay.

She turned to me with tears streaming down her cheeks. The guilt in me for putting her through so much pain and letting down her hopes for my future was gnawing away at me. She kissed my forehead then turned around to leave. I watched her until the door banged shut before I released a few tears of my own.

Chapter Two

~~~~~⊖~~~~~

Shackled, we rode in fear in the back of the sheriff's car. There were three of us being transported to the prison that day from the Henry County jail, and we were not too happy about it; especially after hearing all the rumors about the harshness pertaining to prison life.

We rode mute for about twenty minutes before the deputy broke the ice.

He asked us if we wanted a cigarette.

The deputy had made numerous trips transporting county inmates to prison; he knew what it took to slow the nervous jitters. The guys, on each side of me, accepted a smoke, I guess to calm their nerves, but I declined. I was never a cigarette smoker.

The deputy then asked us which radio station we listened to. All three of us blurted out *Hot 105.7* in unison. It was six thirty in the morning and the only thing playing were slow jams and oldies, which only saddened the mood rather than uplifting it.

There was a song that came on halfway through our destination that pertained to saying goodbyes and missing your loved one(s). Mark, who sat on the left side of me could not take it anymore and broke down. He babbled and cried hysterically about leaving his mother, fiancé, and his two kids behind. In a normal situation, I would have told him to stop acting like a bitch, only the song saddened me as well, but not to the point of crying. We were going to the big house. A place where tears could lead to an anal probe.

Weakness did not exist within me.

Survival was the order of the day.

Our moment of sadness was eventually broken by the nervous fear as Kilby State Penitentiary signs began to appear along the highway. The deputy began instructing us on what we would have to do once we entered the Kilby back gate. No amount of instructions could have prepared us for the treacherous prison that lay estranged from the rest of the world. Several off-white-colored guard towers loomed above the prison, bulletproof glass was encased in each tower along with a walkway that allowed the guards to circle the towers, looking for any suspicious activities.

It did not take long to find out that the guards in each tower were equipped with a rifle for long range shooting and a shotgun for close range—mainly to blow the back out of any unsuspecting violators willing to press their luck trying to escape.

Twelve feet of fencing topped with deadly coils of barbed razor wire designed for shredding and mutilating flesh surrounded the prison. It appeared to be an impregnable fortress against the inmates. I would say there was enough fencing to gate an entire suburban community two times over.

When we arrived at the back gate, there was a dumpy officer holding a clipboard. He was awaiting the necessary paperwork from the deputy before opening the gate. After checking off the paperwork, the officer hit a button that opened a chain operated gate.

As soon as the back end of the police cruiser passed through the iron gates, it clanged shut with a cold harsh finality. A fist pounded deep in the pit of my stomach, clutching my innards, as fear began to set in. I glanced first at Mark then at Chris who both sheltered wide eyed expressions as the reality of entering the prison walls began to thump us in the chest.

The deputy stepped out of the cruiser, stretched his long slender frame and then opened the back door to let us out. The bitter cold November wind greeted us instantly. Mark slowly inched out first, then me, then Chris. The frail white coats given to us at the county did not afford us any protection as the lack of lining allowed the stiff breeze to penetrate ferociously.

We were led up a small flight of steps and into a dim, cavernous room. It was crabbily furnished with one ashen brown desk and a faded white line that marked where the newly acquired prisoners stood.

Dust motes hung suspended in the air and the funky stench of musk, stale cigarette smoke, and unwashed bodies punished my nostrils. The scent came from the other county jail inmates that arrived ahead of us, reeking with fear.

Four stern faced officers sat behind the wooden desk chatting about their bored, washed-out lives.

A hushed stillness engulfed the room…the moment the officers noticed our entry. The deputy walked over to the officers and handed them our papers. He said a few words to them then turned around in our direction. We stood silent while he removed our shackles. The cold steel clattered to the floor like a million bare bones clattering against each other in a wind tunnel.

When he finished, he gave us one long sorrowful stare. "God bless you, youngsters. Life is about to get real, so, pray up," he advised us as he exited the building.

The officers opened our files and called out our names. This was not the standard procedure, but a nosing process the officers did for the sake of knowing what kind of inmate they were dealing with. A large barrel-chested officer with beady eyes instructed us to drop our bags that contained all of our belongings from the county jail. His voice was raspy and stark as he informed us of the officer that would come in to shake us down.

"Whatever y'all do, don't move or say anything until he says so. And please don't take off anything until he directs you to because this guy still thinks he's in the military, not to mention he is paranoid and crazy."

I glanced at the other officers' present who seemed fearful for us except for one stone faced officer who did not mind telling us how he felt.

"You, young punk, tender foots ain't shit. Out here committing crimes and acting like gangstas. You niggas lucky I wasn't the one you did something to cause I woulda knocked y'all heads off wit my forty. Hard out dere in dem streets but ya come in here and think we posed to jump in front of a knife to save y'all asses. Ya criminals and I hate criminals. Personally, I don't give a damn if all ya get fucked in here. Cause all y'all ain't shit, but low life busters. Get out, come back. Get out, come back. Same old niggas. Life don't mean shit to street niggas and y'all niggas don't mean shit to me."

Anger fluttered through every bone in my body and it took all I could muster to keep from stepping over the line and punching his teeth down his throat. Just as I was contemplating some irrational thinking, a loud, gruff voice boomed through the entrance and rattled against the cold stone walls. Mark, Chris, and I faced each other with puzzled expressions as the voice loomed again in the same rhythmic military drone. I averted my gaze to the entrance just in time to see the source of all the nonsensical hollering.

Piercing deep set eyes, a broad nose and a face contorted with rage sat atop a thick neck and wide shoulders. The uniform was ashy blue—the result of too many washes. His pants legs were tucked in his shiny, jet-black boots. He wasted no time in getting down to business.

"Alright everybody, my name is officer Thompson and I don't have the patience for ignorance. I'm gonna tell y'all one time and one time only what to do so pay attention."

His voice was strict and commanding as he orderly directed us through taking off our clothes. Once we were naked the other officers present instructed us to raise our arms, genitals and tongue. They then told us to raise our feet and spread our butt cheeks. This was clearly the most humiliating thing I had ever endured. We remained naked while officer Thompson went through every piece of our property. He discarded everything except our shower slides, bibles, and some hygiene products. Everything else went into a large garbage bag held by an inmate who quickly disappeared, supposedly to destroy the property. I had already heard from a guy at the county jail that everything was sold inside the camp, which proved to be true.

After putting our clothes back on, we had to gather up what was left of our property, which pretty much was nothing at this point. We followed officer Thompson to another processing room. This was when the fear really stepped in. As we stepped out of the first room, all the inmates that were behind the fence stopped doing what they were doing and turned around to taunt us the entire walk over to the next room.

Inmates were whistling, shouting all kinds of obscenities about fresh meat and joking over who was going to have who. I glanced over at officer Thompson who sported a silly smirk on his face. He walked extremely slow and enjoyed every bit of it. We finally reached the second processing dorm which was six times the size of the first dim room. The dorm was brightly lit with a long desk at the entrance. Three caged areas lined the far left of the wall. One held clothes and laundry bags. The second cage held state issued shoes, belts, and jackets. The last cage consisted of three long benches for a makeshift holding unit.

A barbershop was in the back next to a wide-open shower area. The entire room was buzzing with officers and inmates that worked in the processing dorm. A huge, swarthy man with a block shaped head approached us with a clipboard and called out our names. He was wearing a white uniform but his demeanor was every bit that of a corrections officer. After checking every one off, he ordered us to stand in one of the white squares in front of the desk so that we could be stripped searched all over again—including the prowling of the anus once more.

This time was even more humiliating than the first because there was way more officers and inmates in the room. Not only that, but inmates from other counties were being brought in to be processed at the same time. We were a production line of naked bodies being ogled by a warehouse of eyes. This was a homosexual's dream.

We were then ordered to approach the desk one at a time with our property to have it searched again. My guess is the administration expected us to be magicians who could magically make contraband appear and disappear between shakedowns.

This was all the way an overboard and a gigantic waste of time.

The shakedown officers acted like uncivilized barbarians. They screamed every order out at the top of their lungs and dared us with their eyes. I understood the intimidation intent. We outnumbered them so they had to use the slave master mentality to let us know they were the masters. In reality, the inmates could take over the prison whenever they wanted. This watered-down approach would only last if the conditions inside the camp remained favorable.

We stood butt naked in a line while each one of us was led to the shower area where an officer stooped with an insecticide spray can. Yeah, that's right, the exact same ones that pest control agents use when they spray for bugs. Our entire body was soaked in the freezing cold spray. We had to spread our anus and bend over so they could spray it to. Anyone with pubic lice or any hair lice was sure to be free of them after that process. It was at this moment where I began to sympathize with farm animals. We were being herded in just the same, humiliated at every turn and prodded by human hands. We were on display at a slave's auction block because the seasoned convicts were already silently betting and buying up their inmate property.

The shower was identical to the ones that line the beach: long steel pipes with a nozzle on it that sprayed out cold water only. Hot water was nonexistent. We were given a quarter size broken off piece of hard state soap to rinse off with. Each shower was timed for one minute. The cold water stung every inch of my body like a prickly cactus. I was given a medium sized torn towel with rust spots and tattered edges to dry off with. Once dried, I was handed a brown bag that contained two pair of state issued boxers, two extra small t-shirts, a pair of socks and an old-fashioned belt like the ones that came free with a pair of cheap shorts.

After putting on a set of under clothes, I was ordered to the three cages and given a tight-fitting jacket, one set of state pants and shirt, and a pair of state issued shoes that looked like a bootleg version of the first converse all-stars. I put on my uniform that was to define me for the next decade or so, then sat down on one of the benches in the third cage until all the inmates from the other counties had gone through the same dreadful process I had just endured.

Mark was next in line behind me, going through the same torturous process of being sprayed with the bug spray when a booty bandit from permanent party walked in. It was obvious that all the officers knew him from around the camp. They showed him a lot more respect than us newcomers. The officer that checked our property asked him what he wanted, and these were his exact words:

"I'm lookin fa me a job and I know y'all got something fa me back here wit all dese fine ass men up in heah naked with big dicks."

The officer asked him what job did he want to do and he blurted it out with pride.

"I wanna spray nutts and butts all day long. Big dicks swangin in a bitch face don't bother me. Y'all officers already know dat so don't start trippin."

At the mention of operating the spray can, the unprocessed inmates all widened their eyes in protest. Raucous laughter bellowed from the officer before he replied.

"Noooo. Hell no. I can't let you do dat. The way you'd be sweatin dese guys, it wouldn't take long befo one of 'em mops the floor with ya."

"Well, if I can't spray nutts and butts then I might as well leave from back heah so I can find me a job elsewhere. I don't wanna do nuthin else back heah but dat."

He pranced out fuming about not getting the job and the dorm erupted in, "I wish a nigga would talk." A bunch of shit talking with no action behind it.

While waiting in the cage, one of the barbers called my name to get my haircut and a bald-faced shave. This was the part I really dreaded. They were about to cut off all my hair that I had nourished and taken care of for seven long years. I got up slowly and walked sluggishly to the barber chair. I plopped down hard, anger and frustration vividly showing through my body language. There was none of the usual *how do you want your haircut* questions asked. It was just several strokes with the clippers from the front to the back—completely against the grain and growth of the hair. This was pure military. In two minutes, it was all over. No line-up, no dusting off the hair. Get out the way so I can get to the next man. I then had to shave every bit of facial hair off my face.

The barber handed me a razor staff so ancient and Precambrian that I was damn well positive that my great granddad had never seen the model before. It was pure steel with a broad curved head that screwed on and off the steel handle. Once the head is screwed off, you have to place a double edge razor in between the two plates then strategically screw it back together. I looked around to see if the officers were looking then stepped over to the barber and asked if I could shave with the clippers. He must have felt sorry for me because he handed them to me without hesitation. I ran the clippers over my face until the skin began to burn from rubbing the heated guard several times over the same spots on my face.

Finally, I was through with the whole process and all I had to do was wait for everyone else to finish.

When the last man was processed, we had to line up behind officer Thompson so that we could be led to the temporary dorms that everyone must go through for testing before being placed in inmate population. Mike was directly behind me. He was almost unrecognizable because unlike me, he used the ancient be-header razor and cut himself in more places than one could count. He was caricature looking with the blood red tissue sticking all over his face and neck. I wanted to laugh but officer Thompson would have more than likely shown out on me.

We walked in a single file line to the East dorm with only a brown bag containing all the property we owned: a wooly blue blanket, two sheets and a combination lock for our property box. I could hear loud chattering well before we arrived. At the entrance was a desk, curved in the shape of a U. it was big enough to accompany six people comfortably.

A round headed officer with a receding hairline and a haggard face sat behind the desk. At the sight of us approaching, he stood up, six feet tall with inches to spare. He took over the group procession and officer Thompson turned around to head back to the processing room. His voice was languid and nasal like when he introduced himself as officer Jackson. He explained the rules of the dorm, putting heavy emphasis on the no smoking part of the rules.

"Look heah guys, I don't give a shit if you smoke or not. When you see someone smoking ya betta tell'em to put it out cause if I smell smoke, I'm gone make everybody suffer."

I knew then that the temporary stay in east dorm was going to be pure hell because there was no way to stop a heavy smoker from getting his nicotine. After going over the rules about all the new tests, we were going to take and pass before we were allowed to move to population, officer Jackson pulled out a box containing toothpaste, soap, and toothbrushes. The name of the toothpaste was *Spring Fresh*, the cheapest toothpaste in the world in my opinion. No one in the free world would use it, even at gunpoint.

Upon receiving our toiletries, we were instructed to enter the dorm, find our assigned bed numbers, and prepare them in inspection order.

Before I got a full step into the dorm, a blazing inferno heat wave slapped me across the face. The repellent odor of heat coupled with the stench of sweaty, unwashed bodies assaulted my nostrils with the cutting power of a chainsaw. I took one look in the dorm and thought I was stepping into an illegal sweatshop. It appeared to be over two hundred bunks crammed into a building built to withstand only half that population. They were shoved so close together that it was damn near impossible not to smell the next man's underarms. To make matters worse, the noise level was deafening.

The tumultuous chattering of two hundred voices made it difficult to even hear myself think. The television was on but not audible to the human ear because the men playing dominoes in the T.V. area kept up quite a racket. They were slamming down the dominoes and vouching about who was the best. We all know thirty arrogant male egos, all vying to be the best can be noisier than a Mexican bar fight.

I pressed on to the back, looking for bed seventy-two. Sweat popped out on my forehead in tiny beads and raced down my face, only to dive off my chin like an Olympic swimmer. Angry eyes stared me down as I passed through the narrow aisles that were crowded like high school hallways during class change. There was no way possible to make it to my assigned bed without brushing up against someone. With the heat flaring, every brush was subject to lead to near pandemonium.

I finally located my rack, which was a top bunk. I dropped all my belongings into my property box so I could get my bed in inspection order before the dorm officer came around to inspect. The mattress was barely an exercise mat. It was Nile green and thinner than a waffle. The bodies of perhaps a thousand inmates before me had compressed the mattress to its current size. Most of the cotton was torn out in places. The edges were completely shredded, making it difficult to make up according to specific guidelines.

My underarms had become clammy with sweat and my shirt clung to my body like a leotard. We were not allowed to take off any clothing or lay on our racks until after three-thirty. My only relief came from soaking my washcloth in cold water and rubbing it all over my face, neck, and arms.

Privacy would not be possible because the bathroom area was wide open. There were five toilets, which in prison they are called shit jackets. They line a long wall with only inches' distance from each other. A long piss trough was located directly in front of the shit jackets. It would be quite humiliating for the man using the shit jacket. To keep from smelling the man's ass who is taking a piss, he would have to sit up erect and lean his head back as far as possible to keep the butt cheeks from his nose. Lord forbid the man pissing takes a diarrhea fart in your face.

The shower area consisted of five showerheads and a wall that was waste high. It failed tremendously to stop shower hawks from assaulting you with their lustful stares. The bathroom area was always overly crowded with men smoking cigarettes and shaving. A thick fog of smoke hung suspended in the air due to lack of air circulation. It was stifling inside. A California smog confined to an area the size of a football field. No one seemed the least bit concerned about health. The only salvation from the second-hand smoke was to go out of the side door. That was not much relief either.

The fenced area was the size of a small storage shed. It was littered with trash and scores of cigarette butts. If eight people went out the door at the same time it would have been overcrowded.

A claustrophobic feeling engulfed me. There was no solace anywhere. I tried to watch a little television but the loud chattering drowned out all the sound. Mark and Chris were the only guys I knew in the dorm so I straddled over to where they were sitting. They fared no better than I. Sweat glistened on their face as they tried to find some comfort to ease the sweltering heat. Mark was fanning himself with the back of a notebook with no relief from the heated air. We started discussing deplorable living conditions of the dorm when the entrance of the dorm swung open.

Officer Jackson stepped in with a scowl on his face, hollering at the top of his lungs.

"Cut dat fuckin T.V. off and everybody get on yo goddamn rack. I told y'all no smoking in my dorm and y'all got da whole bathroom area lit up like a Christmas tree on fire back dere. I could smell da smoke all the way up at my desk. Now I know ain't nobody gonna admit to smoking so all y'all gonna suffer. I don't wanna see anybody off they rack unless they using the bathroom. If I ketch ya I'm gonna slaughter yo ass."

He got ready to turn and leave, then paused.

"Y'all gone stay dere till I say get down and I don't won't ya layin down either. I want ya to sit up on yer rack."

The door slammed shut with a loud bang. The moment the door closed everybody started talking at once about what they would do to officer Jackson if they caught him in the streets. This was way worse than sitting in the T.V. area. Our blankets were made of cotton and wool. The heat trapped between my ass and the thick wool felt like an oven warming by the minute. Sticky sweat glued my boxer shorts to my butt and a heavy, musk was becoming even more pungent.

This was a stint deep in hell. A place that appeared too distant for the grasp of God. How in the world was I going to make it through a week of this shit? I thought to myself.

One would think the dummies would have learned their lesson, but not quite ten minutes later the sound of matches striking on match boxes could be heard. Officer Jackson came back in the dorm a few hours later to tell us to get ready for chow. By this time, we were all reeking with soiled sweat and musk. This was to be my first meal in prison and my stomach was rumbling for nourishment. The last meal I had was at 5:30 AM in the county jail. I felt like I could eat a dinosaur. Those voracious hunger pains did not hesitate to let me know I was running on empty.

At the mention of chow, the dorm hastily became the equivalency of a bull run in a small Spanish town. Everyone was pushing, hollering and jockeying for position at the dorm entrance to be the first ones to eat. I did not line up until the first group of wild hooligans had already exited the dorm.

While walking to the chow hall, officers were screaming at us the whole time to stay on the right side of the hallway. It felt like kindergarten all over again. The chow hall line was long but it was moving rapidly. I could hear officers screaming out time limits at the inmates who were already eating. A kitchen worker handed me a tray and I followed suit behind the line in front of me. Each server placed a different item on the tray so it operated like an assembly line. The meal consisted of a pale pink hotdog, a crusty black meat patty, hard roll, overcooked peas, spinach and two brick hard cookies. I know it sounds half-way edible but it was unfit for a dog.

I poured some un-discernible drink from a battered cooler in my cup then sat in the section for east dorm inmates. As soon as I sat down, a round body female officer began screaming.

"You got four minutes' east dorm. Four minutes or whenever the first man to sit down is done eating.

Whichever comes first. Shove the food in ya ass fa all I care. Just hurry up so we can get the next dorm in here."

I split open the dry roll and placed half the burnt patty and a hot dog on each half, then took a huge chunk out of one side. It was beyond disgusting. A seasoned turd would have given it a run for its money in a blind taste contest. Pieces of bone gristle and what looked like ground up heart valves hung out the side of the meat like displaced cauliflower. I was starving at the moment. Famished would be a better term.

Yet, I was still debating whether to eat or go hungry. Before my mind started to rationalize all the concerns and gross reasons not to eat, I shoved peas and cookies in my mouth to cover the horrid aftertaste of the meat patty.

"You got two minutes' east dorm. Hurry up let's go, let's go." the plump officer shouted.

Now I understood why the guys were jockeying for a spot in the front of the line back at the dorm. The first to get seated has a couple more minutes to eat than the rest of the group.

There was no way I was going to eat enough to get full if I did not hurry up. I grabbed the murky brown drink and took one long swig before putting down the cup. The drink was grimy tasting but I swallowed it down to move the lump of food caught in my throat.

"Alright, east dorm, get your trays and get outta heah now. Time is up. If you ain't finished, well, tough luck."

Some of the men were still trying to shove a few straps in their mouth. Ms. Pudgy bolted over to their table and started yelling curse words in their ears. The men jumped up and stumbled over the rusted white metal tables trying to get out before other officers could get there to assist her. Kilby fostered a beat down culture. Meaning you can get your ass smashed and slaughtered just because the officers felt like showing off.

We could not leave the chow hall until all of the dorm inmates had turned in their trays. Everyone had to line up single file at the chow hall entrance and exit out at the same time. Once we were in the hallway, the three officers who were waiting for us with latex gloves on began shouting orders at us.

Another strip search.

The third of the day.

By now, all of my complexities were slowly stripping away. We were ordered to take off our socks, shoes, and unbuckle our belts and pants. The officers grabbed the top of our pants and viciously shook them up and down to determine if we had smuggled cigarettes or other contraband in our pants. They spun us around as they finished and told us to stay in line as we marched back to inferno.

Officer Jackson allowed us to cut the T.V. back on and opened the side door to let in some fresh air. Despite the stark solid shakedown, some of the men still managed to sneak in cigarettes and matches they got from their homies who were already in permanent party. Once again, the bathroom was packed to capacity with the smokers. The hazy fog was back hovering in the air in no time. It did not take long before officer Jackson returned and placed us back on lockdown. This time we were on it until the shift ended.

I became so angry with these crash dummies. But there was nothing I could do except suffer the wrath of the punishment. The smokers far outnumbered me so I decided it was best to hold back on my smart-ass comments. All of my energy was used trying to fan myself to stay cool. A lethargic feeling overwhelmed me and in ten minutes, I was fast asleep. I did not give a damn whether I got in trouble for laying down.

Sleep was the master of the moment.

CHAPTER THREE

The same heat that had put me to sleep earlier woke me later that night. Sweat bubbled up on my forehead like carbonated bubbles in a shaken Sprite bottle. Drops had pooled in the crease of my upper lip. The showers were running at full blast, and trapped steam elevated the dorm's temperature. A line of people waited for their turn, while others walked around in their boxers, preparing to shower. There were easily two hundred men in East Dorm, but we were only given one or two hours to shower.

I jumped off my rack and stripped off my sweaty clothes in almost one fluid motion. Though quite a few people were ahead of me, I got in line before time ran out. Missing a shower would have left me as a foul-smelling inmate. In this place, body odor could earn you a beating just as quickly as staring an officer in the face.

All I could think about was a cold shower to cool down. The water was hard, and the soap barely lathered, but I savored the seven minutes of cold relief. The soap's lack of moisturizing agents left my skin ashy and bone-dry. Officer Thompson had thrown away my lotion at the back gate because it wasn't in a clear bottle, so I had nothing to soothe my parched skin. Many men used shaving cream as a substitute for lotion. I tried it, and though it worked initially, my skin became sticky like glue traps. Still, it wasn't itchy or flaky anymore.

I brushed my teeth with thick, gooey toothpaste that tasted like a failed science experiment. Despite using hot water, it clung to my teeth in clumps. Taking advantage of my cooled body, I rushed back to my rack to get some sleep before the heat resumed its grip on the night.

At 3 a.m., the lights blinked on, illuminating the dorm against the pitch-black windows. Another officer had replaced Officer Thompson, but I hadn't noticed the shift change. This new officer had a perfectly round, slightly bald head and a chubby frame that made him hobble as he walked.

"Some security," I mumbled, thinking about the disasters he likely couldn't handle.

"Everybody, get up and get dressed for breakfast! If you're eating, you've got ten minutes!" he yelled, repeating it a few times before sitting at the dorm's front.

I brushed my teeth, washed my face, and lined up behind the stampede. Even at 4 a.m., officers in the hallway screamed at us to stay on the right side. Breakfast was two large brick-like biscuits, watery grits, plastic-looking eggs, and a small meat patty identical to the dinner version. Three officers in the kitchen barked time limits, rushing everyone to make room for the next dorm. I shoveled food into my mouth but struggled to swallow quickly. I avoided the meat patty, though others devoured it like ravenous wolves.

No matter how fast I ate, the four to five minutes slipped away. As the officers screamed, "Time's up," I crammed one last spoonful of grits and eggs into my mouth before beelining to the dishwashing window. I still received a tongue-lashing for lingering a few extra seconds. It made me feel powerless, like a stray dog skulking in a backyard for scraps. After every meal, we endured the same shakedown. Despite these checks, men from the permanent party came in three or four times daily with cigarettes for sale. Some paid with hygiene items, extra clothing, or even shoes, while others promised future payment in unspeakable ways. It was disheartening—a stark reminder of street junkies chasing their high.

I managed to fall asleep but was awakened two hours later by Mike, who reminded me we had to be out of bed by 6:30 a.m. A good night's sleep seemed impossible if you wanted breakfast. I smoothed the thick wool blanket over my rack before a female officer burst in, screaming for everyone to take down their clotheslines and make their racks according to guidelines. "Any clothes left up will go in the trash!" she announced.

Sure enough, she returned five minutes later with latex gloves and a garbage bag. Sweating visibly, Officer Grant checked every bunk. Her loud, shrill voice grated on my nerves. She paused by my rack, scrutinized it, then moved on. After her inspection, she picked five men to clean the bathroom and floors while herding the rest of us outside to a cramped fenced area. Barely large enough for a quarter of the dorm, it held more than half of us, while the rest stayed in the TV area.

At nine, a runner announced the names of those scheduled for tests. We all lined up to be tested for STDs, HIV, and tuberculosis. The nurse drew blood into thin glass tubes labeled with our names. By the time we returned to the dorm, it was time for lunch.

Officer Jackson came on at 2 p.m., and the day repeated itself: smokers clouding the bathroom, Officer Jackson locking down the dorm, and relentless heat turning the cement walls into a kiln. The only difference was the wait for test results. Those tested sat in tense silence, knowing results came within hours. If someone tested positive, masked officers would remove them during the night. Men with HIV or AIDS were sent to Limestone Correctional Facility for treatment, while those with tuberculosis were isolated in see-through cubicles at the dorm's entrance. Their isolation and masks marked them as spectacles, watched by the rest of us. Officers served them through a slit in the door, gloved and masked to prevent an outbreak.

In prison, no news was good news after 24 hours of testing. Mike and Chris repeatedly asked me about the results, both nervous and scared. That night, fear gripped us all. We stayed awake, watching for the masked officers. Like children on Christmas Eve, we anxiously awaited morning. I drifted off but woke to the creak of dorm doors. "Oh, shit," I mumbled, seeing the officers. They looked like executioners.

Most inmates were up, watching as the officers moved through the aisles. They knocked on one man's bunk, giving him two minutes to pack. A low wail escaped him as they rushed him out. The quarantine team left swiftly, tossing his belongings into hazard bags. "Silent ninjas," I thought, finally laying down for a peaceful sleep.

Officer Grant's shift began at 6 a.m., as expected, with her yelling and trash bags. I folded my damp clothes and stored them in my property box. The shirt and boxers I washed carried the faint smell of mothballs, like an old house.

After the dorm was cleaned and inspected, a runner announced names for fingerprinting. Ten of us were led to the processing room to have our prints scanned into the criminal database. We returned, only to be led off again for tuberculosis tests. The shots were relentless. I hated needles and only endured them under duress, but now I had no choice.

At the nurse's office, we waited impatiently as he chatted with an officer, ignoring us. Thirty minutes ticked by, anger simmering silently under the fear of reprisal.

The two officers watching over us stood staring with ferocious eyes, ready to pounce on the first person who dared to speak in the hallway. Signs lined the walls, boldly stating *No Talking*, yet the plump nurse carried on a conversation loud enough to fill a packed stadium. The still, quiet air shattered as two officers approached from the far end of the hallway, shouting repeatedly, "Lockdown! Lockdown!"

The officers guarding us barked instructions. "Alright, this is how we gonna do dis. I want everybody to stay just like you are until I say lockdown is clear. If I catch anyone turning dey heads around, I'm gonna try my best to knock it off ya shoulders."

The hallway fell silent except for the shuffle of feet and the shrill scraping of chains dragging across the cold, hard floor. The ominous sound signaled the approach of a prisoner from the segregation block, likely being transported to the healthcare unit. Lockdowns were meant to prevent attacks on segregated prisoners. The officers escorting such inmates needed to stay vigilant, as their lives were at risk, especially if there was a hit out on the prisoner.

The chains grew louder, signaling the prisoner's approach. After thirty tense seconds, the clinking reached us, then stopped as the prisoner was escorted back toward the segregation block.

"Lockdown is clear," one of the officers announced. We hastily resumed our seats on the hard, uncomfortable benches.

An hour passed before the nurse began calling names for tuberculosis testing. Nervous glances darted around the group, as the thought of testing positive in prison was both devastating and humiliating. A positive result meant immediate quarantine, with all personal belongings confiscated and burned. Quarantine consisted of a small, transparent cubicle at the front of the processing dorm.

There was no privacy, and the inmate had to wear a mask at all times. Quarantine inmates were allowed only an hour outside their enclosure daily, a quick shower in the segregation unit, and a brief phone call.

As inmates exited the nurse's office, they rubbed their arms to ease the sting of the injection. Any rough contact with the injection site could result in a false positive—a nightmare for anyone. When my name was called, I snapped out of my nervous trance and stood. The nurse asked a few routine questions about allergies before administering the shot in my right arm. Afterward, he turned back to his paperwork without a word, dismissing me with a wave. Even the medical staff was rude in this prison hellhole.

Back at the dorm, I sought out Chris and peppered him with questions about TB symptoms. He'd been down before and knew the signs well: swelling or redness around the injection site. That night, I took extra care not to scrub my arm in the shower, checking it obsessively for symptoms. Everything seemed fine. Mark came over to chat for a bit, but the stifling heat soon made it unbearable to do anything but sleep.

In the early hours of the morning, a guttural wail yanked me out of sleep. The noise came from the back corner of the dorm. Squinting into the dim light, I saw a figure convulsing violently on a top bunk near the bathroom. Before I could process what was happening, the man's body jerked over the edge and hit the concrete floor with a sickening thud.

"He's having a seizure!" someone yelled.

I jumped off my bunk and ran toward the commotion. The man's bunkmate had already turned him on his side to prevent him from swallowing his tongue. The dorm lights flickered on, momentarily blinding me as three officers burst in, expecting a brawl.

"Ain't nobody fighting! Someone's having a seizure back here!" a voice shouted angrily.

The officers' aggression softened into concern. One called for a stretcher while the others assessed the man's bloody head wound. Two nurses arrived with a stretcher, moving with maddening indifference. By the time they reached him, the seizure had stopped, and the man was regaining consciousness. His dazed eyes blinked open to find a crowd of inmates and officers hovering over him.

The officers ordered us to step back as the nurses lifted the man onto the stretcher. Blood soaked the sheet under his head, a grim testament to the injury he'd sustained. As the nurses wheeled him out, the dorm erupted in angry chatter. Most inmates were outraged that a man with medical issues had been assigned to a top bunk.

The uproar ended abruptly when the dorm officer stormed in, yelling, "Shut up, or I'll leave the lights on all night!" He slammed the door so hard it echoed, silencing the room temporarily. But as soon as he left, whispers and low voices resumed. I rinsed my face with cold water in the bathroom, then returned to my bunk and fell asleep.

The next morning, I woke groggy and irritable from lack of sleep. Officer Grant arrived, screaming as usual, threatening to drag anyone who refused to get up. We went through the routine dorm inspection, then were herded to the fenced-in yard while the dorm cleaners worked.

Later, the runner came to escort those tested for TB to the entrance. I glanced at my arm, praying it looked normal, and lined up. The nurse walked down the line, examining each arm. He paused briefly when he reached mine but moved on. By the end, three men were pulled aside for further testing.

False positives were common, but further testing meant x-rays and another week in the hellish east dorm. The thought alone made me shudder.

After lunch, we underwent the usual shakedown, but instead of returning to the dorm, officers took us three at a time to a small room near the segregation block for a strip search. We were ordered to remove our clothes, spread our cheeks, and lift our genitals.

One guy was caught with three roll-up cigarettes in his shoes. I shook my head, amused by the ordeal over something so trivial. Nobody got into serious trouble; we were simply sent back to the dorm.

By then, the dorm was noisier than usual. A new group of inmates had arrived, replacing those sent to population earlier. Most of the chatter centered on one of the new arrivals, whose reputation preceded him.

A homosexual resembling a woman had been assigned to a bunk in the middle of the dorm. The chatter wasn't about his sexuality but the fact that he had real breasts and floppy butt cheeks. Many of the guys were astonished to learn about male feminization through shots and pills.

Shower time that night was chaotic. Some acted childish about sharing a shower with a man who had feminine features, while others craned their necks to sneak a peek. The individual seemed to enjoy the attention, lingering in the shower longer than necessary. As he dried off, the dorm's funny men shouted jokes. "Oh now, cupcake, let me put some icing on those breasts," one yelled. Smiling, he sashayed to his bunk, exaggerating his hip movements like a bow-legged woman.

That night was like a comedy show. The dorm comedians kept everyone awake with jokes about the homosexual, who retaliated with zingers of his own. At one point, he claimed the loudest joker would be the first in line for a favor from him. The dorm erupted with laughter and taunts. Finally, in the early hours of the morning, the noise subsided, allowing some sleep.

Barely had I closed my eyes when Officer Grant stormed in, her usual grumpy self, yelling for everyone to get up. As much as I wanted to ignore her, I knew better. A group of officers would barge in moments later, nightsticks in hand, ready to enforce compliance.

The runner came in shortly after, calling names for psychological testing. The test, consisting of 300 questions, was designed to assess our mental stability for assignment to either general population or the mental ward at Bullock County Correctional Facility. When we returned, our group was called again, this time for educational and literacy testing.

We were led to a trailer beside the chow hall. Relief washed over us as we stepped into the first air-conditioned room we had experienced in weeks. We all agreed to work slowly to savor the cool air. The tests were reminiscent of high school end-of-year exams—easy but tedious.

Three test levels determined our grade placement. A pre-test graded by computer assigned us to the appropriate level. I scored high and joined four others in the advanced group, while the rest tackled easier booklets. Some intentionally scored low to prolong their stay in the air-conditioned room.

The weekend crawled by, stifling and dull. At times, the oppressive heat made me feel claustrophobic and on edge. Only the fear of severe punishment from ruthless officers kept me from snapping. To pass the time, Mark and I began a nightly push-up routine before showering. By the time we finished, the shower area was usually empty, allowing us a refreshing cold rinse.

Monday finally arrived, the day I had been anticipating. Cleared of all testing, we were set to transfer to general population, a far more relaxed environment compared to the suffocating East Dorm. In population, smoking was overlooked, food was more accessible through canteen draws, and officers like Grant were nowhere in sight. No more fenced-in morning herding or constant lockdowns.

The morning dragged unbearably. I tried organizing my property box and volunteered for cleanup duty, but time seemed frozen, mocking my impatience. Finally, the runner entered with a clipboard, announcing new dorm assignments based on our crimes. Violent offenders were sent to North or West Dorms, while non-violent ones went to M or G Dorms. I didn't care if they placed me with serial killers—I just wanted out of Officer Grant's oppressive domain.

Chapter Four

Due to the nature of my crime, I was placed in West Dorm along with fifteen others with similar cases. Once we were packed and ready, we lined up behind a frail officer and marched quietly through the hallways. Each officer we passed scowled at us, their lips twisting into menacing grins, as if resentful we had made it through East Dorm.

Before we reached West Dorm, loud swearing and grimy voices echoed down the corridor. It sounded like one of those old prison movies where chaos reigned unchecked, with constant fighting and bloodshed. Chilling visions of blades and gore flashed through my mind. I prided myself on being tough, but this scene was unsettling. West Dorm housed the state's most violent offenders—killers, robbers, rapists, gangsters, and thugs. Survival would require vigilance and keeping to myself.

The skeleton key clicked in the iron door, and all eyes turned to size up the new arrivals. West Dorm was starkly different from East. The rusty twin racks lined the walls as usual, but the shower area, oddly, was at the front of the dorm. There were no partitions—just exposed bodies in full view, like an auction block, vulnerable to prying eyes and potential predators. The piss troughs and toilets sat uncomfortably close to the showers, with barely any separation.

The officer instructed us to find our assigned racks and prepare them for inspection. Navigating through the overcrowded dorm was challenging; even the central aisle had fifty additional beds crammed into it. As I passed, some wannabe tough guys stared me down, silently claiming whatever was in my bag. I met their stares with a smirk, silently daring them to try. The exchange of glares spoke volumes without a single word.

My rack was by a heavily barred window. Sunlight pierced the pale gray light of the dorm, illuminating floating dust motes. The open back door leading to the yard was a stark contrast to the lockdown conditions I had grown used to. I made my bunk quickly and stretched out, staring at the ceiling as sleep tugged at my eyelids. Suddenly, an iron grip yanked my ankle. I shot upright, fists clenched, ready to fight. Relief washed over me when I recognized the familiar chuckle of my old friend, Damarion, or Lil Dee.

Damarion and I had grown up in the same city, though in different neighborhoods. We attended junior high and high school together before he dropped out to pursue the streets. His criminal path had led to juvenile stints and now prison. It had been over two years since I'd last seen him. He looked taller, bulkier, and stronger, though his boyish features remained.

We caught up for about thirty minutes, talking about life in prison and the streets. When he finished explaining how he had adapted to prison life, we decided to walk the track and reminisce further. The dorm was chaotic, with the TV blaring at full volume yet barely audible over the noise. As we made our way outside, heads turned to size us up.

The yard was even louder. Inmates from both West and North Dorm, about 400 in total, crowded the small, grassless yard. A 15-foot-high fence topped with razor wire surrounded the area. A guard tower overlooked the yard, and an officer paced its railing, watchful and alert. Groups of inmates walked the dusty track, while in the center, basketball games stirred up a cloud of dust. The games were heated, with players yelling and arguing over every play.

Despite the chaos, the sunshine and relative freedom felt invigorating after East Dorm's oppressive confines.

The heat didn't bother me; it felt like a blessing. I wanted to burn off the energy with a basketball game and asked Damarion to join me. He frowned.

"Hell naw, man. I ain't gettin' into that shit with them fools," he said.

"Why not?" I asked.

"Man, don't you see how they argue over every move? Prison basketball ain't like the streets. It's the quickest way to get hurt or end up in a fight. You want to lose your teeth?"

Hard-headed as always, I ignored his advice. "Man, you're just acting scary. These dudes don't seem that bad."

Anger flashed in his eyes. "I ain't scared. I'm scared of 45 days in the hot-ass seg unit for knockin' one of them fools out."

Realizing I wouldn't convince him, I joined a game with players from the losing team. The game unfolded exactly as Damarion predicted. Cheap shots, elbows, and shoves turned the court into a warzone. Despite the hostility, my team maintained a two-point lead. On the final play, I faked out my defender and sank a jumper. As the ball swished through the net, a broad shoulder rammed into my gut, sending me sprawling onto jagged rocks.

Pain seared through my palms as I caught myself, but anger drowned out the crowd's cheers. I jumped to my feet, fists clenched, and turned toward the guy who had fouled me. He backpedaled, stammering, "That was a mistake, dawg! You bumped into me!"

His smirk infuriated me, and I charged, ready to swing. Before I could reach him, someone grabbed me from behind. I spun around, fists raised, and met Damarion's piercing gaze.

"I told you what would happen," he said, shaking his head. "You just a hard-headed fool."

"Fuck that punk!" I shouted, still seething.

"Let it ride, man. It ain't worth going to seg and messing up your prison record. You've got a violent crime, nigga. The parole board's never gonna let you out if you keep messing up. You can't do time trying to prove you're king of the cage here. No matter how much ass you beat, niggas will still try you. You've got to chill, like I told you, if you want to survive. And these officers are looking for action. A good nigga bucking like you is prime time for them blue suits."

I glanced at the tower guard, who was watching us closely, then back at the punk. He still wore that smile, acting like he'd won a cage match against a champ. Everything in me wanted to go at him, but my future freedom depended on my behavior. I chose to let it go. Damarion grabbed my elbow and ushered me off the dirt court. I backed away, coldly staring at the punk. He stared right back and smiled, nodding like he was up for round two later. I hoped so—I was still deciding whether to let it ride or sneak him after the officers made their rounds.

Damarion and I walked the track until my anger simmered down. The sky turned a dull gray as clouds covered the sun. We, along with a few others, began heading back to the dorm. It felt cool in there without the sun beating down through the barred windows.

As the heat faded, the dorm grew quiet. Even the television became audible. I was about to head to the TV area when one of the prison runners came in, calling my name. I practically ran to the front. Getting my ID felt like earning a driver's license. Without it, you were just a nameless inmate. But with it, you could buy from the canteen, which was like a mini retail store. They sold everything: hygiene products, snacks, sandwiches, ice cream, cigarettes, radios, even drugs and muscle supplements.

Once you had these items, you gained bargaining power. The hustlers in each dorm sold outside items, phone time, extra clothing, drugs, and more. I immediately filled out a store slip. When the officer called for chow, I didn't rush to the chow hall. Now that I could choose what I ate, I took my slip to the canteen for my daily draw and grabbed some cheeseburgers and pastries on the side.

Jealous eyes followed me as I walked back to the dorm. Inmates without outside support often turned to violence to get these luxuries. They took from newcomers or offered "protection" in exchange for food or store items. Some gangs ran rackets, charging for safety and robbing property boxes for extra cash. It was a dirty game, but I wasn't going to pay for something my family worked hard to send me. I could handle violence if it came to that.

As I opened my property box to store my items, I noticed a few inmates eyeing me. They quickly looked away whenever I made eye contact. I rushed to stash my stuff, not wanting them to see what I had. I mentally marked each one as a potential suspect if anything went missing.

Damarion pulled me aside to explain box break-ins. "Having a combination lock is the same as having no lock. These guys can open a lock with a piece of a coke can in seconds." I was furious. The money on my books was mostly spent on this store, and I couldn't risk losing it. "Calm down," Damarion said. "Just buy a key lock off the store next week. It costs about eight bucks, but it's worth it. No one's getting in with a key lock."

I wasn't totally satisfied with this, but it was a step up from nothing. For now, I kept my stuff in Damarion's locked box. The next week, I bought a key lock. It wasn't foolproof, but it was better than a combination lock.

The first few weeks in West Dorm followed the same routine: up at 6:30 a.m., out of the dorm until 8:30 when the cleaners finished. Damarion and I kept doing our daily push-ups and walking the track. The only real change was the basketball court. I stayed off it, but I enjoyed watching the violent games.

I soon learned that most people came to watch the fights, not the game itself. Whenever an argument broke out, the crowd would gather, urging the tension to boil over into a fight. It was like the Roman coliseum, where the crowd cheered for blood. Even I found myself drawn to the sideline, anticipating the violence. No matter how violent the games got, once the fight was over, they went right back to playing as if nothing had happened.

By the third week, the weather changed rapidly. From hot, long days to windy, cool ones. The rain came in torrents, and most people hated the rainy days. When it rained, we were stuck inside, crowded together in the humid, musty dorms. Trash cans were set up to catch leaks in the roof. The mix of rainwater and trash created a foul stench, adding to the discomfort.

After three days of being cooped up, nearly everyone stormed the yard when the officer opened the door. The wind howled, but I hesitated to go out. The smell from the trash cans was so bad, I almost stayed in. But fresh air won out, and I joined the others on the yard.

The dirt track, once sandy brown and swirling with dust before the rain, was now slick orange mud. With the paper-thin soles of the state-issued brogans, it was only a matter of time before someone would injure themselves. Sure enough, it happened—worse than expected. Nine people were playing a warm-up game of twenty-one on the dirt court before team ball. The tramping and jumping created a slick slush, and clay-colored mud clung to the ball, making it heavier than usual. Whenever it hit the rim, it bounced farther than expected, causing the accident.

A young, rambunctious teenager was at the free-throw line. He bent his knees slightly before releasing the ball too forcefully for the distance. The ball hit the back of the rim with a loud thud, and the backboard rattled. A light-skinned guy with red hair and freckles dashed after it. By the time he grabbed the ball, he realized how close he was to the razor wire. To avoid running into it, he slid feet-first—an impressive move, like a major-league steal. But this slide wasn't to win a game; it was to save his life.

The razor wire vibrated with a sound like mating rattlesnakes. The freckled guy's face contorted in pain as he let out a sickening scream. His pants ripped, and his right leg split open like a melon. Blood pooled under his leg. The razors had cut almost to the bone, exposing his flesh. Tears streamed down his face in rhythm with the blood. By the time the stretcher arrived, he had passed out from shock. Healthcare workers rushed him to the hospital, hoping to save his ankle.

After the blood was covered with dirt and the scene calmed, the game resumed as if nothing had happened.

That night, I received paperwork from the classification specialist about my permanent transfer. Although I had started adjusting to my temporary stay at Kilby, I was ready to leave. The same environment each day made time drag. I needed a change of scenery. Little did I know, where I was headed, I might've been better off staying at Kilby. By the end of the fourth week, homesickness consumed me. Visions of broken family ties and deferred dreams plagued me day and night. Some days were more emotional than others. The lack of activities didn't help. Food became my only comfort, and I stuffed everything I could afford into my growing waistline. I dreaded every phone call home, and afterward, I would sit in a daze, wondering about the future of my kids, now being raised without a father. I prayed they wouldn't become another statistic, trapped in the penal system with no hope.

Tuesday of the fifth week, I was awakened in the middle of the night. A burly officer wearing latex gloves tapped my foot. The sight of the gloves filled me with fear, making me think of health-related issues. But when I saw his face unmasked, I relaxed, realizing it wasn't a health scare.

"Get dressed and pack up your stuff. You're transferring in the morning," he said.

Packing by moonlight slowed me down, but I could hear the other inmates preparing to transfer. The officer returned, rushing the process. Five minutes later, we were lined up in the hallway for roll call. There were twenty-two of us transferring to a new penitentiary by first light.

After roll call, we went through processing again. Grumpy, red-eyed officers screamed and ordered us around, checking our property for contraband. We were strip-searched once more. When they were done, we were sent to the sick call room to wait for the transfer van.

The sick call room was cold and bleak, with rust-colored vents blowing stale air. The walls were pockmarked, and the benches were scratched. The room felt like a mental institution. I sat in the far corner, pulling my jacket over my head to avoid the cold. The air was frosty, and my teeth chattered. Some inmates slept fitfully, others complained about the harsh conditions. Before long, our voices filled the room until a fiery officer appeared in the doorway.

"I could hear y'all all the way down the hall," he screamed. "Don't let me hear a peep outta you until the transfer unit arrives. Shut the fuck up."

After he left, a few inmates grumbled, wishing they could take him on. Two hours later, the officer returned to escort us back to the processing center. We were divided into groups based on our destination. Eleven of us were loaded into each van. Those serving life sentences were shackled completely—leg irons, belly chains, and handcuffs. The rest of us were only shackled with leg irons and handcuffs.

We were packed into the van like sardines. The drivers didn't care how tight we were, urging us to load up faster. The leg chains dug into my ankles like razors as we squeezed in. Our property was stuffed into the van, crammed into our laps or under our feet. There wasn't room to turn our heads. The pain was intense, but I wasn't scared—just nervous, like a stray dog trapped by a dog catcher.

Most of the guys had been to prison before. They talked about their previous incarcerations, boasting about fights or stories of hate. One guy spoke about the fifteen extra years he got for assaulting an officer after serving twelve years of a life sentence.

Exhausted, I drifted off to sleep after about ten minutes. The position I was in caused pain in my lower back, waking me up. A sign passed that read "Elmore County." Ten minutes later, we entered a lush green valley, then the scenery shifted dramatically. Endless railroad tracks and piles of rocks stretched to the horizon. Graffiti covered a train caboose with dozens of boxcars waiting to be loaded.

About a quarter mile further, we turned onto a twisting back road that led to a minimum-security prison. Surrounding it were two medium-security prisons, where I was headed. The towering fences and razor wire made it clear that these were secure facilities. Guard towers stood watch, completing the oppressive scene. The colorless landscape felt like an artist's rendering of despair.

We turned right onto a rugged road that led to Draper's back gate. The sight of the prison was stark, with the same cold, grim architecture. I was about to enter this place, a prison community surrounded by others. A whole world built for one purpose: imprisonment. It felt like a massive, profitable system designed to perpetuate itself.

Chapter Five

The van made an abrupt stop in front of a massive gate, which was slowly opened by a white-clothed prisoner. A pudgy officer sat behind a sturdy wooden podium, waiting for the driver to hand him the necessary files on each inmate being transferred. If not for the seriousness of the situation, I might have laughed hysterically at the officer, who looked as though he were lost in time. A thick, bushy mustache swallowed his upper lip, and his hairstyle resembled the Soul Glo commercial from Eddie Murphy's *Coming to America*—dripping wet, curly, and long. The collar of his thick blue coat was soaked from the gel dripping off his jheri curl. He looked like a real old-school country boy, as out of touch as the convicts who had served over twenty years. At that moment, I sensed we were in for a rough haul.

Five of us were dropped off at the Draper back gate. The other six were headed to Level Five and Six supermax camps. The pudgy officer instructed us to enter a shabby concrete structure connected to the back gate. Once our cuffs were removed, we grabbed our laundry bags and shambled inside.

We entered through an incredibly small, dust-clogged office. A tiny desk sat beneath a dingy, stained window, its surface littered with strewn papers and a greasy black telephone. A grill-less air conditioner wheezed and hummed in the other window, barely circulating any air across the room.

The officer opened a heavily scarred wooden door that creaked noisily on its hinges. It led to the back of the building, which was in even worse condition than the office. Two long wooden tables were placed side by side. The only lighting came from the faint daylight that filtered through the dirty windows and the open door, which was blocked by a locked metal grate. Against the back wall were two cages, large enough to house three grown lions. The weak light barely illuminated the dark interiors of the cages. One cage contained several water coolers and a single toilet, while the other had two wooden benches braced against the wall.

The officer directed us to the left cage and ordered us to remain seated until he returned to strip-search us. We crowded into the cage, struggling to fit with our property. Even though I wasn't close to the toilet, I could smell its rank stench. I held my breath for as long as I could, trying to avoid inhaling the urine-scented air.

After what felt like an eternity, the officer returned with a stone-faced colleague. We were led out of the cage to endure another strip search. By this stage, most prisoners are immune to strip searches. I no longer felt embarrassed about being naked in front of strangers.

Once we were thoroughly searched, the officers dumped our belongings onto the floor like trash, inspecting every item for contraband. Then they left us to sort through the mess. As one officer went through my property, he began shaking his head.

"What's your name, son?" he asked.

Recognition gleamed in his eyes when he saw my last name. It turned out he had family from my hometown and even knew some of the same people I did. A frown tugged at the corners of his mouth when he learned I had a fifty-four-year sentence.

"Son, how in the hell did you get fifty-four years for a robbery on your first offense? Hell, over half the guys in this prison got two or three robbery charges apiece and way less time than you. You must've done some crazy shit to piss them folks off in dat courtroom."

I shrugged before answering, realizing that the day the gavel struck, I'd been given a raw deal.

"Well, sir, I took a chance with an appointed lawyer. Plus, the predominantly white county where I was sentenced treats Black criminals like toys. Once we mess up, they throw us away without a second chance."

"You're too young to sit down wit all dat time over your head, youngsta. You need to get another lawyer to reduce dat sentence so you can get home to your family."

I nodded in agreement. This was the first officer I'd encountered who showed genuine compassion. I suspected he had a relative or friend who had been through the system—someone who had taught him to see inmates as human beings rather than animals. I was about to thank him for the encouragement, but the other officer barked at us to gather our property and move on.

We were led to another caged holding pen, this one much larger. Half of the cage was sectioned off with braided metal wire, behind which hundreds of soft drink cans were piled high—some crushed, others intact. Someone was clearly making a fortune recycling the commissary's discarded cans. On the other side of the wire, two water coolers sat on a metal shelf.

A weathered wooden signpost bore the words *SALLY PORT* in large black letters. Beneath it, a set of rules outlined inmate conduct for those assigned to Sally Port duty. From our vantage point, part of the prison yard was visible. It was ten times the size of Kilby's small dirt track yard, with two full-sized basketball courts and a massive weight pile on the left. The right side was blocked from view by a few dorms resembling army barracks.

Despite the biting wind, the yard was full of inmates. Most were shooting hoops or lifting weights. I squinted toward the basketball court, searching for familiar faces, but saw none. The only thing noticeable from this distance was the near-fights and constant arguments erupting on the court. Vulgar obscenities echoed as the winning teams taunted the losers.

"Ain't no way I'm gettin' on dat court wit all dat heatin' and jaw jackin' goin' on," someone behind me muttered.

"Fuck dat court. How long dey gonna keep us out here? Shit, it's colder than a deep freezer out here," the tallest guy yelled angrily.

Almost as if hearing the complaint, the pudgy officer reappeared and ordered us to follow him.

Walking down the hall with our property bags in one hand and the mat draped over the other arm was tedious. Inmates from other dorms stared and smirked at us, as if we were fresh meat and they the snarling wolves. Near the end of the hallway was Dorm Two, the most populated cell block in the entire prison.

"This is where y'all gonna sleep," the convict said, shaking the steel-barred door violently. Moments later, a haggard officer shuffled lazily from the back of the dorm and unlocked the heavy door. He didn't speak or make eye contact as we entered. For him, it was just another day of new "wannabe thugs" arriving to be broken in.

The dorm was a chaotic blur. A blind man would have struggled to distinguish it from a rap concert. A group huddled around a guy pounding out a bouncy beat on a metal property box. One by one, they took turns rapping, cheered on so loudly by their friends that their words were barely audible. The beat was flawless, better than anything Dr. Dre could have produced.

Elsewhere, domino games were in full swing, with players boasting and bluffing as loudly as the rap group. The upper tier was just as noisy. I couldn't imagine what they were doing up there with only one officer overseeing over two hundred inmates.

The dorm quieted briefly as people stopped to size us up, their piercing stares probing for signs of weakness. The convict pointed me to a bed rack at the front of the cell. I was relieved not to have to navigate the rowdy crowd with my property and the weighty mattress slung over my arm. Beneath my bed, an older Black man was playing dominoes with a younger guy. Back at the county jail, repeat offenders had warned me that older bunkmates were far better than young gladiators. The seasoned convicts demanded respect and often looked out for their bunkmates, unlike the rowdy younger inmates.

Hoping the older man would be my bunkmate, I tossed the tattered mat onto the top rack and bent down to ask which one I'd be sharing the space with. The younger guy glared at me like I was dirt on his lawn, but the older man glanced up from his dominoes and said, "That's gonna be me, youngsta."

Relieved, I introduced myself. He told me his name was Willie, and he was from a small town called Clayton. "Oh yeah?" I said. "That's just ten minutes from my mom's hometown in Eufaula."

The mention of Eufaula piqued his interest, and he forgot about the game. Willie began peppering me with questions about people he knew there. To my surprise, we knew several of the same folks. The younger guy, clearly annoyed at the stalled game, stomped off to the top tier after shooting me a fiery glare.

Willie, unbothered, continued talking. Within an hour, I knew everything about his hometown. He then switched gears to prison life, offering survival advice.

"A lot of these old-timers prey on new tenderfoots like chicken hawks on baby chicks," he said.

"Well, I ain't gotta worry about that," I replied. "Ray Rivers came to prison a man, and Ray Rivers gonna leave prison a man." I spoke loudly and clearly, hoping anyone entertaining ideas would hear me. From the back of the dorm, someone let out a sinister laugh.

"What the fuck's that supposed to mean?" I yelled. No one replied. Willie told me not to take the bait.

"Man, you go back there and swing on one of them youngstas, and half the dorm's gonna jump you. They're clicked up and ready. You ain't got a name here yet, so lay low and avoid trouble. Ain't no one-man islands in here."

Willie was right. I learned my first survival tip: few men in prison fight or stand alone. Without the backing of homeboys or a gang, a man could be pressured into vile acts.

"Just lay back and pay attention to your surroundings," Willie advised. "You'll learn who to fuck with, how to work the system, and how to get what you want."

I knew he was right, so I vowed to stay low-key and vigilant.

Later, I picked at the terrible dinner, then ventured out to the yard. The temperature had dropped, and most inmates stayed inside to avoid the wind. Only the die-hard lifters braved the elements. The icy gusts kicked dirt in my face and stung like fire ants. My thin state-issued jacket offered no protection—it was like wearing a garbage bag.

The weight pile was nearly empty, with just eleven of us out of a potential thousand inmates. The others were bundled in gloves, skullcaps, and makeshift facemasks. I grabbed a 45-pound plate, but the icy metal burned my hands. When it slipped and clattered to the ground, a muscle-bound lifter called out, "Take it easy, youngsta. This all the weight we got. You wanna grind with us?"

I glanced at their bent bar loaded with excessive weight and declined. Instead, I grabbed dumbbells and completed a few burnout sets before the cold drove me back inside.

The dorm was almost as cold as the yard. Some fools had opened the windows, welcoming the bitter gale like a refreshing breeze. Willie sat on his rack, sipping coffee mixed with hot chocolate.

"What's going on, youngsta?" he asked.

"Nothing much—just cold as hell out there, and it ain't much better in here."

"You better get used to it. It's gonna be like this all winter," he chuckled. "Some of these idiots never had a house on the outside, so they don't know how to act with a window. They slam it up and down all day like they're in a car."

I laughed and sat on his rack to challenge him to a game of dominoes. Willie beat me soundly, but I enjoyed losing to him. He cracked jokes the whole time, sharing stories about the crazy things he'd seen in prison.

As night fell, the day's light seemed to vanish into a void. A starlit sky briefly took its place.

"You might wanna shower now," Willie advised. "Later, it's gonna turn into a freak fest back there. That shower wall's a motel room for them."

Taking his advice, I headed to the shower area. An icy blast hit my chest as I turned the corner. A massive hole in the wall had been fitted with a fan spinning at full speed. I stared at it, shivering, until a bumpy-faced white guy walked by and said, "That's how they get the steam out."

"Steam?" I yelled. "You mean frost because that's all that's back here! This doesn't make any sense."

"I don't get it either," the bumpy-faced guy said, "but that's their explanation for freezing our asses off back here."

In my head, I guessed the prison authorities did it to keep inmates from hanging behind the wall engaging in sexual activities. We had to turn all the showerheads on full blast to create enough steam to shower without freezing. After five minutes, my teeth were chattering uncontrollably. The arctic gale overpowered the steam and hot water. I rushed to finish showering and dressed as quickly as possible.

Willie took one look at my frantic expression and burst into loud laughter.

"I forgot to tell you about that freezer back there, youngsta. But I guess it's too late now!"

"Yeah!" I replied. "A little late for a warning."

Willie's smile faded into a grim expression. "Well, I forgot to warn you about the shower area, but I got worse news for you—if you think that bathroom is bad."

"It can't possibly get worse than that shower," I said.

A frown crept across his face, like he was about to deliver bad news about a death in the family.

"I hate to tell you this, youngsta, but you might wanna get yourself some shut-eye. They'll wake you up first thing in the morning for the job board. Everybody who comes to this camp, no matter their age or physical condition, has to get a job. Ain't but two options for newcomers: kitchen or farm. All the kitchen slots are filled, so you'll most likely end up on the farm for a hundred and twenty days before you can switch jobs."

My jaw clenched in anger.

"Farm?" I shouted. "Ain't no way in hell I'm going out there in this frostbiting weather."

"Oh, you're going," Willie said. "It's either the farm or the lock-up unit. Both are fucked-up choices."

"So, they just treat us like slaves for a quarter of the year with no sympathy?"

"Basically, yeah. All the greedy higher-ups care about is swelling their fat accounts off the cheap, backbreaking labor of inmates. They'll have you picking hundreds of thousands of vegetables and clearing acres of land while they hunt prize deer on the same property. Prison is an institutional hustle. Corrections is on the stock market now. Incarceration is big business, especially for those building all these private prisons popping up everywhere."

I shook my head. From the setup of the system, it was clear every word he said was true. Fuming with anger, I lay back on my rack and worried myself to sleep.

In the dead of night, I awoke from a violent dream to a bladder throbbing with pressure. I sat up, adjusting my eyes to the panther-black dorm before jumping down. The downstairs officer was slumped over on a metal bench in the TV area, his head bobbing up and down as he fought sleep. Upstairs, the officer was probably doing the same.

Halfway to the bathroom, I noticed several nocturnal prowlers roaming the dorm. A sulfuric yellow light glowed eerily at the bathroom entrance, casting shadows in the far corners. A hulking figure stood in the entryway, arms crossed over his chest. He looked like a praetorian guard of ancient Rome. Something felt off, but my bladder was screaming for relief.

As I approached, I heard a smacking sound echo from the back of the bathroom, like a pimp slapping his whores. I moved to pass the hulking figure, but he stepped in front of me, blocking my path.

"What's your problem?" I asked angrily, meeting his cold, coal-black eyes.

"Somebody's handling business in there," he said.

"I don't care what business they're handling. I gotta piss like a racehorse, and I'm not waiting for some chump to finish screwing a punk."

"Go upstairs, then," he replied.

"I sleep downstairs. I'm using this bathroom," I said firmly. I wasn't about to back down. Giving in on my first encounter would have marked me as weak for the rest of my time here.

Realizing I wouldn't turn around, the man dropped his arms to his sides, readying for a fight. I was about to barge past him when the sound of a toilet flushing broke the silence. A thin inmate emerged from the shadows, grinning ear to ear like a Cheshire cat. Two sweaty, rough-looking men followed, smug satisfaction etched on their faces. As they passed, a stench of sweat and hair grease filled the air.

I pushed past the guard, making eye contact as I entered. He walked off but kept looking back at me. At the farthest toilet, I relieved myself, keeping an eye on the entrance. After finishing, I cautiously checked for anyone lurking in the shadows. Satisfied I was alone, I returned to my rack.

I stayed awake for an hour, ensuring everything was calm before finally drifting off to sleep.

Chapter Six

BAM BAM BAM! CLINK CLINK CLINK!

"What the hell?" I yelled, bolting upright. I tossed my blanket aside in one swift motion. Angry, confused, and ready to fight, I cursed loudly and was about to unleash more choice words when I saw the beefy officer standing by my rack, holding a broom and a set of skeleton keys.

"It's time to wake up and get that rack in inspection order," he barked in a rough, cocky voice.

Groggy and fuming, I snapped back. "Is beating a man's rack the only way you know how to wake someone up? That's childish as hell."

He retorted, voice even harsher than mine. "You're in my house, son, and with that smart-ass mouth, the next wake-up might be an ass whooping."

I opened my mouth to reply, then thought better of it. Being on bad terms with one officer meant being on all their bad sides, and that could make life hell. Sensing my restraint, the officer smirked and moved on, pounding every rack he passed even louder than before.

I wiped the grit from my eyes and jumped down to brush my teeth. Gray light filtered through the barred windows, hinting it wasn't yet six a.m. On my way to the bathroom, the clanging of keys against racks continued, accompanied by muttered curses from inmates behind the officers' backs.

By the time I finished brushing my teeth, Willie was sitting up, a baffled expression on his face.

"What's wrong with you?" I asked.

"Out of all the prisons I've been to, this is the only camp where officers beat on racks with brooms and keys. Some days it's hard to tell who's more ignorant—the officers or the inmates. They both do some crazy-ass shit."

"You're not lying about that. I saw some wild shit just last night."

"I tried to warn you about going to the bathroom late. Best bet? Don't drink too much, so you don't wake up needing to piss. In here, you gotta train yourself to survive. Crazy shit happens late at night, and people lose their lives over dumb stuff. You gotta be careful."

I nodded in agreement, but stubbornly, I still didn't like bending to prison rules. After making up my rack to inspection standards and dressing, a lanky administration runner entered the dorm with a clipboard. He stopped by each rack, telling those who had been at Draper less than three days to report to the chapel in five minutes for orientation.

Orientation featured a poorly made video with interviews of the warden, captain, and classification specialists. They explained penitentiary rules in barely audible voices. Next came a second video showing inmates being assaulted for failing to repay debts or favors. We laughed at the cheesy dramatizations—snacks left on bunks, then eaten, leading to violent payback—but deep down, we knew some of the men laughing would fall victim to these games.

We received forms for phone privileges, visitation, and funds. The next morning, everyone who attended orientation was called to the job board over the loudspeaker. The same lanky runner lined us up alphabetically outside a narrow corridor leading to the ICS office.

As men returned from the office, we nervously asked about their assignments. Every answer was the same: farm squad. The only variation was the squad number.

When my name was called, I stepped into the office, shocked to find the warden himself assigning jobs. He barely looked up as he spoke in the driest, nasally voice I'd ever heard. "Farm squad seven."

Three words. No questions about my health, mental state, or qualifications. He didn't even glance at my braced leg. My carefully thought-out plan to avoid the farm crumbled. One side of me urged, *Say something,* while the other warned, *It won't make a difference.*

Nervously, I stammered, "Ex... excuse me, Warden. I had a bad car accident before prison. My knee was torn in two places, and I was still in therapy. I can barely bend it or walk long distances."

He grinned—a twisted, paperclip smile. "Well, inmate, we'll see how that leg holds up. If it gives out, we'll send someone to fetch you. Until then, you're on the farm starting today at 12 p.m."

I left, stunned. He was the coldest, most heartless man I'd ever encountered—a short, power-drunk dictator. There was no bargaining. I returned to the dorm and prepared for the inevitable.

At 11:45, the loudspeaker blared, calling all farmers to the back gate for check-out. Stepping outside, I was nearly blown back by the icy wind. Half the camp seemed assigned to the farm. Seasoned farmers were bundled for the weather, but I had no ear or face coverings. The relentless gale slapped my cheeks and froze my ears until they felt ready to snap off.

Willie didn't work the farm, so he lent me his coat. Even with two jackets, the cold was brutal. My thin pants offered no protection from the biting wind. I shoved my fists deep into my pockets, trying to preserve some warmth.

Many of the men were dressed for battle against the elements: long johns, layers of jackets, gloves, and makeshift face masks crafted from torn shirts and socks. I swore to myself that I'd never face the cold so unprepared again.

The air crackled with static as the squad officer shouted names over a microphone, ordering us to line up in pairs. There were seven squads, each assigned to different plots of land. As we marched out of the gates, the wind hit even harder.

"Goddamn," I muttered. "Now I know how cavemen felt sleeping outside."

Farm bosses, heavily dressed and armed, rode atop sturdy horses, barking orders. Pump shotguns rested by their saddles, with chunky Glocks holstered at their waists. It felt like a scene straight out of the pre-Civil War South.

The only difference was the few white faces among the squads and the modern weaponry.

There were thirty-six men on farm squad seven: two keg men carrying the water cooler at the front, four deuce leaders maintaining formation, one flagman with a tattered squad flag, and the rest of us—the plantation workers. The keg men set the pace, lugging the heavy cooler ahead of the line.

"Alright, squad seven, let's pull it," the farm boss ordered. We marched behind two other squads to a tool cart overloaded with rusted, prison-made tools. The deuce leaders distributed the gear—half received digging hoes, the other half sling blades. The tools, crude and heavy, were welded metal pipes with dull blades. Thinking it easier to manage, I grabbed a sling blade but soon regretted it. A thin layer of ice coated the rusted metal, adding to its cumbersome weight.

Equipped with tools, we set off on a grueling trek to a bleak stretch of land. Walking in formation, stride for stride, our cheap, thin-soled boots scraped noisily along the ground. The deuce leaders barked orders at those lagging behind, ensuring we kept pace. Passing cars whipped icy winds into our faces, compounding the misery. Twenty minutes later, we arrived at a hard dirt path winding through black, slushy earth. It led us past a rancid compost site worked by inmates from Elmore Prison. Tractors dumped decayed waste—meat, vegetables, and other chow hall leftovers—into a steaming compost pit. The stench was unbearable, a vile brew that seeped into our clothes and clung to our skin.

Seagulls swarmed the area, shrieking and fighting over scraps. The spectacle momentarily distracted me from the nausea, but the relentless fumes soon had my stomach churning. I fought down bile, unwilling to show weakness in front of hardened criminals.

My hands ached from switching the cold tool back and forth, my frozen fingertips barely functional. The tedious march strained my weakened knee, but finally, we stopped in front of a patch of tall, dry weeds swaying in the wind. A deuce leader relayed instructions:

"Alright, squad seven. Boss says it's gonna be cold as hell tomorrow, so if y'all want a fire, you gotta knock down these weeds and stack 'em in piles to burn. Got it?"

A few men muttered agreement; others cursed under their breath. The deuce leader assigned roles—those with sling blades would cut down the towering weeds, while those with hoes piled them up.

Grumbling, I stepped into the sea of weeds, cursing my decision to grab a sling blade. The dead stalks loomed overhead like corn ready for harvest. I hacked furiously, the dull blade demanding brute strength to cut through. Cottony residue burst from the pods, resembling snow. My arms throbbed, and raw blisters bubbled painfully on my palms. Lightening my grip to ease the pain, I lost control of the blade, which clanged against another tool.

"Hey, nigga, watch where you swingin' that blade! You hit me, and it's goin' down," the man barked.

"My fault," I muttered, acknowledging my mistake.

An hour later, we'd cleared a large stretch of land, stacking enough piles of weeds to burn for days. We lined up for water, icy cold in flimsy paper cups, which I drank greedily despite the freezing weather. Sweat drenched me from exertion, but as we stood waiting, the cold seeped back into my bones. My teeth chattered violently, and I longed to resume work just to warm up again.

At the end of the day, we reassembled for the long, bitter trek back to Draper. The wind battered us relentlessly, and upon arrival, we lined up outside the shakedown shack. Each squad waited to be strip-searched before entering the prison.

The shack reeked of stale sweat, unwashed bodies, and damp clothes, a repulsive smell reminiscent of my high school locker room. The farm squads flooded in, filling the air with noise and complaints about the harsh conditions. Amid the chaos, "kicking it" began—raucous banter laced with humor and innuendo.

"Lil Roddy, you must've been doin' squats, 'cause that ass is gettin' bigger!" one inmate joked.

"Yeah, much as I been squattin' these nuts in your mouth," Roddy shot back, sparking laughter throughout the room. Even the officers chuckled.

After the search, we stepped back into the freezing cold, allowed only to put on boxer shorts inside. Fully dressing outside felt like a cruel punishment, the wind biting through to the bone. Shivering violently, we rushed to cover ourselves.

By the time we returned to the dorm, dinner was nearly over. I ate quickly and trudged to my bunk, exhausted. Willie, as usual, was perched on his rack, dominating a game of dominoes. He grinned when he saw me.

"What's goin' on, teenager?" Willie asked.

My anguished expression must have said it all because he grimaced as though he could feel my pain.

"Irately, I relayed the day's events, sparing no detail. After I finished explaining the farm experience, he offered to help.

"Well, teenager, if you got a tee shirt, I can help you make something for your head and face."

Without hesitation, I grabbed a tee shirt from my laundry bag and watched as Willie fashioned a face shield from the back of the shirt and a toboggan from the sleeves.

By seven, I was completely worn out from the day's toilsome work. If not for the stench of compound fumes wafting off my skin and the mud caked under my nails, I might have fallen asleep without showering. My arms hung limply as I shuffled to the restroom, dragging myself through exhaustion.

The bathroom was revolting, barely fit for use. Two guys brushed their hair in front of cloudy, toothpaste-marked mirrors, their noses almost pressed against the glass. Shaving cream and powder caked the insides and outsides of the sinks. One sink, clogged with wads of toilet paper, overflowed into a rapidly expanding puddle. On the toilet seats, green, jelly-like mucus wads clung like grotesque ornaments. Someone clearly had bad aim and even less concern. I used nearly half a roll of toilet tissue wiping up the mess, then double-lined the toilet seat before sitting down.

I avoided looking at the filthy wall in front of me and turned my gaze to the floor. Brownish-red and green boogers hung on the walls like macabre decorations. An open sewer drain in the floor emitted a fetid stench, sharp enough to jolt me awake like smelling salts. The only solace was the faint sweetness of soap wafting from the shower area.

After showering and dressing, I huddled near the TV to catch the weather report. We didn't have to check out if the temperature dropped below thirty-two degrees. In the summer, it had to be ninety-seven degrees or above for us to stay inside. The weatherman forecasted thirty-four degrees, but with wind chill, it would feel like twenty to thirty. Half the dorm, myself included, erupted in applause until a few veteran farmers dampened our mood.

"Hey, while y'all clapping, remember, the warden don't always consider wind chill a factor," one of them said.

Realizing the likelihood of checking out, I climbed onto my rack to grab some sleep. From my experience with the stonehearted warden, I knew we'd be headed back to the farm at first light.

A loud whistle startled me awake in the dead of night. The vibrant horn of a train echoed through the darkness. I stared out the barred windows as the midnight-black train rolled past the prison. Its whistle reverberated like the cries of a haunted conductor. The creaking and grinding of wheels faded into the distance, leaving faint vibrations in its wake. I lay back down, wrestling with sleeplessness for another hour.

At dawn, the metallic pounding of keys against the bunk racks jolted me awake. Gray pallor from the dorm lights confirmed it was still early. Groaning, I slipped on my shower slides and climbed off the rack, only to be hit by a thousand spikes of pain in my lower back. I stood motionless until the throbbing eased. My nose had started leaking overnight, and my body felt paralyzed with cold. Around me, everyone else was also getting ready for another backbreaking day.

The weather was unseasonably cold, with a biting wind that cut through my prison-made face covering and toboggan. It was still better than exposing my bare face. Frosty breaths rose from conversations like smoke from brush fires.

Partway through the trek, the farm boss led us down a different path. We passed small state graveyards with crookedly etched headstones. As we trudged along the clay-colored paths, we arrived at a mountain of wooden pallets. I, along with eight others, chose to carry pallets instead of ice-glazed tools. This decision soon proved disastrous. The dew-soaked pallets, weighing nearly thirty pounds, were unwieldy as I hoisted one overhead.

The pallet quickly became a burden. My hands, unable to retreat into my pockets, froze painfully. Passing a brown-green cesspool, the wind intensified, cutting through our coats like knives. The gusts blew pallets out of our hands multiple times, forcing us to stop and regroup.

We veered off the clay path into a vast field dotted with hills. Dry grass and weeds tangled around our boots, causing many to stumble. A steep embankment led us to the piles we'd stacked the previous day.

Six men with hoes dug a trench around the largest pile to prevent the fire from spreading. Pallets were placed at the base and top of the stack, while tissue was wedged into crevices. Attempts to ignite the pile were thwarted by the dew-soaked brush, but eventually, removing the wet layers revealed dry weeds that caught fire.

Crowding around the blaze, I thawed my frozen hands and feet. The heat was both a blessing and an agony, as my face felt like melting wax. When smoke stung my nostrils, I stepped back. Each time the fire waned, we added pallets and brush to revive it. Even the farm boss had his own small fire to combat the cold.

By nine-thirty, the fire was extinguished, leaving us vulnerable to the punishing wind. At ten-thirty, we returned to camp, famished and exhausted. My stomach growled as I devoured my vegetables, followed by a soup, cheese crackers, and microwaved chili in my cell.

Before resting, I heard the heavy pounding of footsteps approaching. A female officer arrived to relieve the acting cell officer. Not knowing what was happening, I observed from my rack and witnessed the perverse practice of "gunning."

In prison, "gunning" refers to masturbating in response to seeing a female officer—or even a new inmate. Some inmates engage in this behavior blatantly, stripping down and masturbating openly. Others do so more covertly, cutting holes in their pockets or tying strings to their toes to achieve climax.

This behavior, rampant in prison, has led to strict penalties, including disciplinary actions and isolation. I made a point to avoid inmates involved in such activities, knowing a tarnished record could prolong my sentence.

Chapter Seven

The entire first winter, I learned more about prison and making bad decisions than I ever cared to know. It did not take long to find out that the people in prison were from all levels of society. Many were highly intelligent, while others were mere groupies and followers. Sorrow and guilt got the best of some men as they worried about things in the outside world that they had no control over. The worst kinds of inmates to get into an altercation with were those whose lives were hardened by rugged lifestyles. These prisoners were cold. Their hearts were eaten away by years of selling drugs, gang wars, and murderous violence. I, too, had come from that world and had been desensitized to human pity and violence because of what it took to maintain a living in the street hustle. The solitude and peace I was experiencing in prison gave me the mental clarity to focus on solutions, not just the problem of what I needed to do to gain my freedom. I was one of only a handful who were being reformed by time.

A few of the violent inmates kept to themselves, but the majority preyed on the weak and fearful, taking what they wanted—sex, food, and drugs. They stuck to the script of surviving by their carnal nature. These men alone were why reformation was hard. They created environments similar to the ones many of us came from, providing all the ills an addict craved—whether it was gambling, alcohol, drugs, sex, hustling, gangbanging, or money. Most inmates did not have financial support from family, so they got deeply invested in the game to earn a living. Violence was often the key determinant in their chances of having a chunk of the pie.

To avoid confrontations with inmates like this, I lived by some very important advice that Willie gave me within my first week in prison. He told me never to let anyone get close because everyone had some kind of angle or edge they were always secretly promoting. This way, they could never figure me out. As long as they could not figure me out, they would not know how to approach me. Therefore, they would shy away from trying anything crazy because they would not know whether I was a killer or just a measly car thief. Even though I kept to myself, there was not a day that went by that I did not catch someone staring at me with vicious, cold, hard stares—evil enough to pierce the gates of hell.

Over the next two months, I observed numerous personalities, quickly learning who to stay away from and who was okay to associate with. Out of thirteen hundred inmates, I only associated with four other guys who were not about any foolishness. They slept in different dorms than I did, so whenever I visited them, I would get this distinct feeling—sort of like being in a different prison every time I entered another cell. This was because no two dorms were alike. Each dorm was a different enclave enclosed within the penitentiary, where the inmates determined how it was run.

On the weekends, men from other dorms would pour into another cell to get in on some illegal activities. It reminded me of being on the strip in Miami, Florida, where you leave one club and walk next door to another with totally different entertainment. The entertainment in prison would start on Friday night and end on Sunday night. Every Friday, we watched one of the latest movies to come out on DVD. After 10:30 a.m., only a few people had to check out for jobs. The rest of the men would be inside the camp, gearing up for the weekend.

Each dorm was assigned two sets of TVs—one upstairs and one downstairs. That meant a hundred or so inmates were expected to crowd around one thirty-two-inch television to watch a movie on both floor levels of a dorm. I'm sure you can pretty much imagine how this situation caused problems every weekend with a bunch of violent men all vying for prime seating arrangements. There were only four wrought iron benches in the entire movie area. First shift did not allow seat reserving, but the minute second shift count was complete, almost every inmate in the dorm rushed to the movie area to claim a seat. They placed bed sheets over half of the bench to reserve a spot for themselves, their homeboys, and their boyfriends. Some inmates tied a shoestring across the bench to claim a reservation. Most nights, the reservations claimed first were respected unless someone new or drunk disregarded the inmate rule and decided to sit wherever he chose. This always ended up in a fight.

Just about every Friday, the same inmates who sat closest to the movie area reserved the exact same spot every weekend. This was when they began to form the idea that a certain bench belonged to them. Bloody fistfights ensued over who had the most rights, as if they were landowners bickering over a property line. The nights when things flowed without issue were okay if a good movie was chosen.

Once the movie started, the self-proclaimed dorm divas made their entrance to the area to join their men.

The fortunate ones would have on real lipstick, eye and lip liner, nail polish, perfume, and altered, tight-fitting state pants that resembled jeggings. All the dorm divas arched their eyebrows regularly, and most of them even went through the non-sterile, painful process of getting their tongues and nipples pierced.

The unfortunate ones used creativity to gain an edge. They used Kool-Aid to make lipstick, ink pens for eye and lip liner, a permanent marker for fingernail polish, and state pants cut into tight shorts two sizes too small. They sat on the movie bench with their boyfriends, eating popcorn and drinking prison-made liquor or peppermint-and-cocoa-laced coffee called a "player shot." These couples kissed and hugged throughout the movie without any other care or concern in the world. This was their heaven reimagined.

When the movie ended, the couples gathered at the back of the dorm with their loudly altered radios and partied like they were in the club. The prison girls popped and twerked their asses as if they were female strippers while their men danced behind them with their arms in the air. These inmates did not care whether they made parole or not. Life in prison was not so bad for them—especially for those who were practically homeless on the streets. Even the men with kids in the free world carried on without a moment's thought of getting out to be deeply involved in their children's lives.

Saturday's entertainment would start with college football or basketball. Sports fanatics would study the sports section of the newspapers to find out the professional predictions and keep up with the injury report of the players. They gambled on parlay boards and tickets, with the odds of winning heavily stacked against their favor. It cost a pack of cigarettes for a spot on the board and prime canteen items to play a ticket. Almost every weekend, some shady guy trying to get over got beat up for putting out tickets and not having the money to pay those who hit big. The quickest way to an asswhooping or killing was through gambling.

There was always so much excitement going on with the games that even the officers placed bets. The street officers known for making moves kept more prison money than the inmate bookies. When the games were over and all money won was paid out, the gamblers would go to different cell blocks to play cards or shoot dice. Dorm hopping was against the rules, but a pack of cigarettes was always the head-nodding bribe. In each dorm, the inmates gambled with different stakes in the game. Some bet huge, while others bet small. No matter what dorm a gambler visited, all the gambling occurred at the top tier. It was easier to position a lookout man at the top of the steps to watch out for monkey officers.

Over half of the dorm would be drunk, high, or rolling on pills by nightfall. Some inmates with the gift of gab could talk an officer into bringing them liquor, weed, crack, or pills. Others made their own gallon jugs of wine called julep. The bootleggers used different ingredients to distinguish their taste from each other—ranging from V8 juice, to Kool-Aid, to sugar water, fruits stolen from the chow hall, raisins, orange Tang mixture, and powdered yeast. They wrapped a thick wool blanket around the jug to make it ferment faster. Most brews were ready by the weekend. One cup cost a pack of cigarettes or two bags of coffee. The alcoholics had money sent to the bootleggers' accounts or by Western Union to an outside family member for gallons at a time. It was a lucrative business that could not be stopped with threats of write-ups and segregation time.

Arguments and fistfights plagued the weekend like an old cowboy saloon brawl. Many younger guys, unaware of prison's unwritten rules, drank with anyone, not realizing the liquor would have to be paid for. Sooner or later, they ended up in debt that could only be repaid with sexual favors. Some wickedly sly men never asked for repayment outright. Instead, they concocted their own version of date rape drugs to gain an edge during a midnight booty raid. Muscle relaxers or psychotropic pills, bought from medicated inmates, were slipped into drinks. When mixed with alcohol, these drugs stiffened a grown man's body to the point of near immobility. Victims remained conscious but had no strength or control to stop the violator from ravaging them.

Some booty bandits even plotted their victims in advance, setting up group assaults on the helpless. So many men were "turned out" during nights of drinking and partying. The same vices that landed them in prison continued to plague their lives in this concrete hell, where one would think a man might develop the mindset to straighten up. Yet, rapes were rarely reported. Broke men with addictions found the trade-off of "booty meat" for sweets, drugs, food, coffee, cigarettes, and other prison items a worthy deal compared to being prideful and waiting on a hopeless money order from a broken family on the outside.

It wasn't hard to tell when a tenderfoot had been tricked out of his ass. The following morning, human excrement and clumpy blood often decorated the floors and toilets. The bathrooms remained filthy until dorm cleaners scrubbed them after everyone checked out for their assigned jobs.

Sundays weren't much different. On the bottom-tier television, white guys watched racing, while mixed crowds of Black, white, and Latino inmates gathered upstairs for football. Since these were professional games, the stakes were high. Almost every Sunday, some knucklehead placed a huge bet without a single item in his box to cover the loss. Some got lucky and won. The unlucky ones either got beat down or packed their belongings in a mad dash to protective custody.

By Monday, the last of the liquor and wine had been drained from cups and jugs because most shakedowns occurred during the week. The first month of my prison term was relatively quiet, but after that, shakedowns became clockwork. The veteran inmates always knew when one was coming. Their connects in the shift office kept them informed about conversations between officers and superiors. It didn't matter which shift conducted the search—the officers tore through everything we owned with relentless fury. I often wondered if they were rewarded with orgasmic satisfaction for destroying our belongings.

Before every shakedown, superiors hyped up the officers in a meeting. They stormed down the halls in full search mode, screaming at the top of their lungs for everyone to get on their assigned bunks. A hushed silence spread through the dorm—no talking or whispering was allowed. Any form of communication resulted in a near-death beatdown. We remained on our bunks until signaled to step down.

One by one, we were stripped naked in front of the entire dorm and given a series of degrading commands to ensure nothing was concealed in our body cavities. It was the most humiliating experience ever—especially the bending over. I could feel the eyes of the booty bandits as I spread my cheeks wide for the male and female officers. The female officers tried their best to mask their expressions, but seeing that many dicks in one hour had to affect their relationships at home. No amount of money in the world would make me comfortable knowing my wife had to witness more dicks in an hour than a porn star saw in a lifetime.

After the strip search came the hurricane. Officers yanked our property boxes from under our bunks and tore through them. Some dumped the entire contents onto the floor, kicking through our belongings like animals. I watched pictures of my kids slide across the dorm floor, memorizing their locations so I could retrieve them after the chaos. I didn't want some pervert stealing my pictures and masturbating to fantasies of violating my children.

Important legal papers that determined a man's freedom were emptied from folders. Photos were ripped from homemade albums. Food items were scattered, and laundry bags were dumped like trash in a landfill. There was no regard for family memorabilia or crucial documents. In the officers' eyes, we were all part of the same animalistic breed, deserving of extinction.

The last step was stripping our mattresses. Officers ripped open any holes, searching for contraband. Trash cans were overturned, spilling rancid juices from discarded food and drinks onto the floor. The dorm reeked of putrid fumes. Those whose mattresses had been shredded had to get replacements, which were no better than the ones destroyed. After the shakedown, we scrambled to collect and reorganize our property boxes.

Venomous smirks and sarcastic claps echoed through the dorm as the officers left. The men knew it pissed them off when they found nothing. Most times, they came up empty-handed because prison had become our home, and we had mastered hiding our contraband. To compensate for their failure, officers resorted to petty confiscations—extra sheets, blankets, laundry bags, cups, or stamped-out clothes—just to appease their superiors.

By the beginning of my third month, I had fully adapted to this new way of life. Things that once sickened me no longer fazed me. I witnessed horrors I had never seen on the streets—men sharing an overused needle, pumping heroin into their thin veins. Heroin was rare in my part of the country, and I was glad for it after seeing how it turned men into zombies, nodding back and forth for hours.

I saw die-hard gangsters sucking tongues out of each other's mouths, attempting suicide or murder over an ass they didn't even own. I witnessed violent gang rapes, stabbings, and massive beatdowns over packs of cookies and cheese curls lost in gambling.

One crucial lesson I learned: never sleep without two pairs of boxers and pants on. I memorized this rule after watching men get their boxers slit open in their sleep. The violators would jack off to their exposed ass cheeks and laugh about it the next day.

Prison was not survivable for cowards or wannabe gangsters who caught cases as flunkies. A strong mind was the only thing that ensured a man walked out of this hell unscathed.

★★★

If not for the highlights of visitation day and the constant encouragement from my loved ones, I would have probably lost my peace and freedom to violence months earlier, given the relentless disrespect inside those walls. Inmates and officers were equally demented, pressing nerves daily. As soon as my visitation list was approved, my family made the very next visitation day. Visits were every other weekend, and I made sure to appear untainted by the system.

Everyone treated visits like a star-studded event. From Monday until visitation weekend, those expecting visitors spent every item in their box to have their clothes pressed, creased, and starched. Haircuts were pristine, with sharp razor line-ups. We sprayed on the most expensive cologne, smuggled in by runners. Shoes were cleaned beyond newness and stored in clear plastic bags to keep them dust-free. I never slacked on my appearance. The moment I laid eyes on my family and kids, I fought back tears as they ran into my outstretched arms. Their familiar scents, smiles, conversations, and pure love transported me down memory lane.

Even the most depraved men in the dorms transformed when surrounded by their loved ones. Hardened inmates who openly slobbered over their prison boyfriends suddenly played the role of loyal husbands when their wives or girlfriends visited. They hugged and kissed their women as if there was no other love in their lives. I felt sorry for the women oblivious to the truth. More than a few times, I saw men so strung out on their prison lovers that they arranged meetings between their boyfriends and their families—wives, kids, and immediate relatives who depended on them. These stunts never ended well. Even children sensed the deeper meaning behind these so-called friendships, and once the façade crumbled, the inmate usually lost his family's full support.

One of the most miserable sights was a man incarcerated in the early stages of his lady's pregnancy. When they finally saw each other, he wouldn't even recognize the child as his until told during visitation. I saw the pained look in their eyes as they silently cursed themselves for not being present in their kids' lives.

The end of visits was the worst. As I walked toward the exit, my little girl clung to my neck, and my two boys wrapped their arms around my legs with strength far beyond their young ages. I couldn't look at them as my family pried them off me. Their grief and tears could have broken me faster than a building demolition. I could avoid their teary eyes, but I couldn't shut my ears to the haunting question they always asked: "Daddy, are you ever coming home with us?"

"No, no… not today, but soon, hopefully real soon," I always answered. The lie burned my tongue every time I tried to soothe them with what I thought they wanted to hear. Barely would I get the words out before they started crying again.

Back at the dorm, while everyone discussed the women on the visitation yard, I lay on my rack, drowning in grief and memories.

As winter faded, so did my 120 days on the farm before I could apply for a job change. Spring arrived with hot, rainy days. In early April, I asked the farm boss to submit a good work report so I wouldn't have trouble securing a new job. The next morning, my name was called for reassignment. I whistled while getting dressed, relieved to finally leave the grueling farm.

In the I.C.S. office, one look at the assistant warden's sinister grin told me something was up.

"Well, it seems all the jobs in the camp are full. So, for now, there'll be no change. Whenever something opens up, you'll be reconsidered," he said, dripping with sarcasm.

His words drove stakes into my heart. A tsunami of hatred surged through me. I wanted to lunge across the desk and wring his scrawny neck until he choked on his own spinal fluids. He must have sensed my rage because his smile disappeared when he looked up. I stormed out, seething with violent anger that could have made me the perfect recruit for a foreign-born terrorist.

The assistant warden was so cruel that he didn't even give me a day's break before sending me back to the farm.

As soon as second-half check-out began, I was called to report to the back gate for duty.

The sun blazed like a magnified heat ray, searing my arms and face. By the time Squad Seven stepped outside, sweat was already beading on my forehead. At the tool wagon, we picked up the scalding hot, heavy metal tools. To the right, the farm boss sat atop his muscled horse, watching us closely. The horse was well-groomed, its hide shining with an oily sheen under the burning sun. The entire scene looked like a museum sketch of a brutal slave plantation at the height of the cotton-picking era.

Before we started, the deuce leader asked for directions. The farm boss, his voice groggy, replied, "We're going to uncharted territory—virgin lands to you rookie farmers."

This was clearly code because the deuce leader understood immediately. We followed Squad Six along a hard clay path past an orchard of pecan trees. In the middle stood a house used to train state dogs for tracking escaped convicts. White trucks with D.O.C. insignias were parked all over, their cages filled with snarling dogs. White-clad inmates picked pecans and trained the dogs—house niggas marveling at the master's Big House.

After the orchard, we veered onto a dirt road stretching for miles. The vast land shimmered in the sun—

rolling hills of grass leading to an endless expanse of pine trees. At the forest's edge, I saw rotting stumps and dried pine needles scattered everywhere. The ghostly white figures of other squads moved through the trees like spirits.

We entered the woods, trudging stiffly through layers of fallen needles. The sweet scent of pine filled the air like incense. Shafts of sunlight pierced through the dense branches, cutting through the forest floor like divine swords. By the time we caught up with the other squads, they were already dragging branches up a steep incline.

Before I could question why they were piling branches in the middle of the woods, the squad leader barked orders: "Alright y'all. Boss man wants us to drag these branches to the edge."

Someone in the back groaned, "Man, I'm too light to be dragging shit heavier than me."

The ass-kissing deuce leader wasted no time responding. "Oh, you gon' drag dem branches, or boss man gon' write yo ass up, add a hundred days mo' to da farm. Ain't that right, boss man on the high horse?"

I wanted to hurl a prickly pinecone straight at his skull.

I grabbed two thick branches and dragged them to the woods' edge. By my third trip, sweat drenched me, and my lower back throbbed. When the deuce leader called for a water break, I nearly cheered. We lined up, almost emptying the keg before it made a full round. The farm boss allowed a ten-minute rest, but I refused to sit. Dusty pine bark was a breeding ground for snakes. I just wanted to finish and hopefully get sent in early.

By 10 a.m., the first half was over, but more grueling work awaited in the second. The piles stood taller than my head.

Drenched in sweat, we stumbled into the shakedown shack like stampeding bulls, desperate to escape the sun's brutal rays. The stench of sweat and musty underarms filled the air, thick enough to choke on. By the time I reached the chow hall, a female officer wrinkled her nose.

"Goddamn! Y'all smell like a hog pen. They had y'all workin' by the damn compound today?"

I smirked. "Oh nooo, they had us sampling cologne at the warehouse."

She shot me a wild-eyed look before checking my number. There was no time for a shower before second-half checkout. I sat on the movie bench, hoping to rest my aching feet. Before the pain could fade, the intercom buzzed. The back-gate officer's voice blasted through: "Checkout for all farmers!"

I cursed loudly, dragging myself to the back gate. The sun was still merciless as we began the long walk back to the farm.

They issued us flimsy white hats at the work site, supposedly to block out the pounding rays of the sun. It fared no better than any of the other prison-issued items. It was so hot they had to run the water keg down the line before we even began working. As soon as the last man was served, we went straight to work.

We were ordered to drag the heaping piles we had stacked up on the first half across a clay path to a designated spot in the field to be burned. A circled trench was dug, and limbs were thrown into the pile. The thickly rounded branches and parts of the tree trunk had to be chopped into smaller pieces before being tossed into the fire. I, along with four other guys, was chosen to hack the limbs while the rest of the squad dragged them across the path to the burn pile.

It didn't take long for blisters to sprout on my palms. The hacking was constant, leaving no time to cushion my hands against the vibrating metal handle. After thirty minutes of swinging the heavy ax, it took its toll on my entire body. A feverish pain throbbed in both my shoulders and the lower arch of my back. The workout was three times as intense as pushing stationary iron. This was a grueling, total-body punishment.

The blisters became so tender that whenever the ax bit into the wood, I could feel a slight trickle of blood as they burst from the impact of the vibrations. Sweat ran into my eyes and down my back. When an entire pile was broken down and ready for burning, the farm boss gave the signal for us to stop chopping. We joined the rest of the squad, who stood as far away as possible from the emanating heat of the fire.

The fire sat atop a grove of wild onions, seasoning the air with an aromatic smell. Once the fire burned out, it was time to gather our tools and head back in.

The following day was one of the hottest I had spent on the farm. The temperature hovered around ninety-six degrees, and it was a dry heat without a hint of a breeze. The heat was unbearable. Standing in the looming shadows of the building offered little comfort because even the shade was scorching. As soon as we stepped out to begin our walk to the farm, the sun reigned its wrath of searing torture.

I could feel it burning through the flimsy bill of my hat. Even the farm boss' horse refused to be out in the heat. Halfway through the trek, it whined and bucked, turning in circles like a cat chasing its own tail. This continued until the farm boss dismounted. As soon as he grabbed his rifle and water jug, the horse raced off at tremendous speed toward the stable. A smile creased the faces of the farmers as they enjoyed the fact that the farm boss was going to have to endure the same grueling journey that plagued us all year long.

He was angry about having to walk, but that didn't free us from the torturous path we still had to endure. Our cheap, thin-soled boots, worn from long winter walks, only added to the pain. I felt every rock as if I were wearing a pair of seventies-model All-Stars. Each stone or crevice felt like a barefoot walk across cement spikes.

The route wound us through a suffocating stench between the compost and the cesspool. A hot breeze blew the fumes straight up our noses. To the left, the warm cesspool emitted an odious stench of human excrement. Off to the right, decayed meat and rotted vegetables from the compost heap released a putrid smell into the air. A rampant buzzing of flies feeding on scummy scraps resonated in the distance.

As I forced back the lump of bile rising in my gut, the stench of the compound raked my throat and stung my eyes. We walked through that shield of funk for about five minutes before the increasing distance dissipated the fumes. The path veered left, but instead of continuing it, we ventured into a dense brush. Thin streams of water poured from a rusty drainage pipe and trickled along a mushy path.

Our boots sank into the swampy mud, making a squishy sound like stomped-on fish guts and eggs. The deuce leaders began barking orders to clear a huge patch of land immediately.

"All right, farmers, we gonna clear out dese bushes, and we gone do it quickly. The faster the brush disappears, the longer rest period we gone have. So let's have at it."

Those of us with axes and sling blades went in first, eradicating the thick brush and small trees swiftly. As the thin trees and thick brush timbered to the ground, the men with hoes raked them into piles.

Large sweat circles decorated the armpits of our shirts as we hacked away at the stubborn overgrowth. When a huge tract of land was cleared, the farm boss allowed us a water break. Some men laid their tools on the ground and sat on them, hoping to keep the moist mud from seeping into their clothes. It didn't work—the tools sank into the soft mud.

Idle conversations carried on but were barely audible as thousands of gnats, mosquitoes, and yellow jackets buzzed around our heads, angry that we had destroyed their habitat. Ladybugs landed in our hair and crawled down our backs, searching for new homes.

Right after receiving the signal from the farm boss, the deuce leaders screamed that break was over. My body was stiff and aching, working against me as I stretched to loosen up for the rest of the day's work.

We deuced up and walked past the cleared land only to stop in front of another dense brush. This land needed a backhoe tractor to clear it. Yet here we were, doing the state's bidding for free—risking heat strokes, snake bites, and angry inmates wielding medieval tools.

Two other squads were in the same vicinity, and they, too, looked haggard and worn—or at least I thought so. Before we could start swinging, one of the youngsters in the squad asked the farm boss something I'll never forget.

"Oh nah, boss, can I get permission to beat me one down from squad eight?"

"Yeah!" the farm boss answered. "You got two minutes to handle your business. You boys know what time it is—put it on the line."

Immediately, all three squads came alive. Each rooted maliciously for the two youngsters to go at it full swing. This was old-school plantation mentality—savages combating each other instead of challenging the system that masterminded these conditions.

The two youngsters, clearly pissed about something from the camp, charged like bulls fighting for pasture dominance. The guy from squad seven threw two wild punches, but the one from squad eight ducked and scooped him up almost simultaneously, slamming him into a prickly bed of briars and weeds. Before the guy could catch his breath, the other sat on his chest and pounded him with blows strong enough to knock the gold out of Mike Tyson's mouth.

The blows were ferocious. The fight needed to be stopped before the loser's face got too messed up to return to camp without triggering an investigation. The farm boss knew this. He ordered the fight broken up before permanent damage set in.

Embarrassed, the beaten youngster stood up, shaking, blood draining from his nose and mouth like a faucet. He grabbed the stick used for carrying the water keg and raised it, ready to strike.

The sharp crackle of a pump shotgun seized everyone's attention.

"Put dat fuckin' stick down, goddammit," the farm boss shouted, raising the shotgun in his direction. "Ain't no weapons gone be used on nobody out here on my time. Everybody checks back in on my squad, and they betta keep dey damn mouths closed about what goes on with squad seven."

The stick dropped so fast it was hard to tell it had even been moved. Two minutes later, everything was back to normal. We resumed work until stopping time. By then, we were completely drained.

As we stepped back onto the hard clay path, sweat continued to rain down my sun-parched face, only to dive off my flesh onto the dry, cracked earth. We arrived at the camp reeking of sweat and funk, the heavy stench of the compound clinging to us like skunk vapor.

I skipped the chow hall in favor of a cool shower and freshly laundered whites. My energy was drained, and I wanted to nap, but my conscience told me to check out a book from the law library. While flipping through a Stephen King novel, I overheard two white guys talking about three job openings for GED tutors.

I shuffled over without hesitation.

A high school diploma and a couple of packs of cigarettes were all it took. I jumped at the offer.

The next day, I was introduced to the GED instructor. We discussed my background and which subjects were available for tutoring.

"Any subject is okay with me, sir," I answered formally. I felt like a respectful field slave trying to get a job in the big house where no hard labor was required. I didn't have on my best Sunday britches, as the good country folk used to say, but I did have on my pressed visitation whites and brand-new Timberland boots to make a damn good first impression. He seemed impressed with my qualifications and eagerly signed me up for the job board the following morning.

The rest of the day was a breeze. Even my time on the farm went by fast as my excitement over the prospect of a job change overshadowed everything. I was leaving the sticky heat and the grueling farm for the cool, air-conditioned tutor job. Gaping stares burned through my back as the farmers wondered in awe about my sudden change in attitude. The dull blade whistled in the air, severing weeds and thick stalks like a John Deere riding mower. Nothing could dampen my mood.

Nightfall was a different story.

As I prepared for sleep, I had dreadful thoughts of the warden denying me the job. Anger swelled as swirling visions of his sinister smile haunted me. Defeated by sleep, I tossed and turned through a violent series of dreams, some more hideous than others. In one nightmare, I was frantically swimming from the depths of a murky lake. Just as the tips of my fingers broke through the surface, a powerful whirlwind detonated from the lake's floor. It gripped my ankles in a vehement hold and yanked me back down into its voracious bowels.

Amid the whirlwind, I realized it wasn't an underwater storm but a contorted, hissing mass of poisonous sea snakes. Thousands of them stretched in all directions, trying to untangle themselves from the knot that bound them. Acid-yellow venom stained their fangs. My legs were tied by unseen hands to the writhing mass, trapping me with no way to escape. Suddenly, the snakes stopped struggling for freedom, their eyes feasting on me, the human intruder. Their mouths opened too wide for their heads, and a shriek of pain and rage erupted from their throats.

I awoke with an atrocious jerk. Sweat gushed from my body like my adrenaline was at max heart rate. As the fear of the dream faded, I blinked repeatedly, adjusting to the clammy darkness. Sweat wasn't the only thing seething from my pores. Urine blasted around inside my bladder like a volcano about to erupt after a century of dormancy. I slipped on my shower slides and fast-walked to the bathroom.

While exiting, I turned my head toward two figures behind the wall separating the toilets from the showers. I caught an eyeful of gruesomeness. A thickly built inmate sat on the back urinal while his scarecrow-framed boyfriend stood in front of him, ejaculating semen all over his face. Sickening, I thought. Lurid acts like this occurred so often in prison that nothing shocked me anymore. I had become desensitized, like a war vet spending a year in a war-torn nation. A blown-off arm is shocking the first couple of times, but after repeated exposure, it doesn't even ruin your appetite. That's how almost every inmate copes with time.

I jumped back on my rack and lay on top of the covers. It was humidly hot, and I was anxiously jittery about my new job opportunity.

Chapter Eight

The warden sat there mulling over his paperwork as if some grave mistake was written on the assigned job sheet. He looked up at me, then back at his paperwork. The creeping smile no longer decorated his face. I could imagine the thoughts going through his head, and I laughed inwardly at my slick defeat.

"All right, Rivers, it looks like you'll be removed from the farm to the G.E.D. building effective Monday morning."

There was pure hatred in his voice, sharp enough to sever full-grown oak trees. Since today was Thursday, keeping me on the farm until Monday sealed his title as the victor. To the warden's ego, he just could not be defeated by some criminal inmate. As I turned to exit the office, I caught a swift glimpse out of the corner of my eye at the slithering smile reappearing on his face.

Because the farmers did not work on weekends, the warden made sure I was checked out for those last two days. When I left the job board office, the farmers had already checked out and were likely hacking away at some unused stretch of land. Before I could get to the cell block, my name was called on the intercom to report to the back gate. Upon arrival, I saw a white truck with state insignias along the sides. Someone had arranged for me to be dropped off at the farm. With no doubt who that someone was, I jumped onto the back of the truck. After stopping at the tool shed, the driver took a brutally bumpy route, speeding excessively for the uneven dirt path. With every bump and hole, I bounced as if the truck bed were a trampoline. Loudly squeaking suspensions rumbled as the driver barreled toward the work site.

Topping a small rise, the farmers looked like machines, working in unison to clear a worthless patch of land. I waited for the truck to stop bouncing before jumping off to another toilsome day's work.

Later that night, rain came down in streaming torrents, slivering down the dirty windows like thin garter snakes. Rain was the most beautiful sound to a farmer because it usually meant no checkout the next day. With Fridays already being a half-day, I smiled at not having to check out on my last day on the farm. Willie and I stayed up late, drinking coffee and reminiscing about the past.

I awoke early to the sergeant's harsh voice hollering over the intercom for all farmers to prepare for checkout. I cursed out loud, joining most of the other farmers who couldn't figure out why we were checking out in the rain. I looked out the barred windows to assess the damage from last night's storm. Smoke-gray clouds melted across the dreary sky, rain puddles and dew covering everything exposed overnight.

"How stupid could they be?" I said to Willie. "Shit, a blind man could tell it won't be long before the rain returns."

"Well, teenager, if you think there's an officer in this whole prison system who cares if you get sick, then you need to pay more attention to your surroundings."

"I ain't say they cared, I just think it's stupid to check us out when it's evident the bottom gonna fall outta the sky within the next hour or so."

"Teenager, all I can say is I done seen plenty of times when the farmers come in soaking wet."

The day started out miserable and ended the same. We trekked through ankle-deep rain puddles and trudged along winding mud roads the color of tangerines. Our cheap boots slid across the slick, wet slush, struggling for a foothold to keep up with the deuce—damn near impossible. Water sloshed against our boots, casting up billows of murky liquid. We ended up at the same dense, swampy woods as the day before.

Halfway through the morning, tiny sprinkles of cold rain began dropping ceaselessly from the stormy sky. The deuce leaders scrambled to get everyone properly deuced up to head back before the rain fell harder. We wasted no time forming up. The deuce line walked at marathon speed, but it wasn't enough to escape the worst of the storm.

A deafening roar of thunder echoed across the smoky sky, and the sprinkles became fat volleys. The faster we walked, the harder the rain came down. It became so heavy we could barely see ten feet ahead. This would have been an escape artist's dream getaway. The rain pounded on, stinging our faces like a swarm of killer bees. We arrived at the shakedown shack bedraggled and drenched. They rushed us through because of the lightning, so we didn't have to strip fully naked. Instead, we remained deuced up in the needle-like rain while the farm bosses patted us down. I felt the water soaking through from my shirt to my underpants to my skin. As soon as the last man was patted down, I sprinted inside the camp.

My fingers were wrinkled like prunes, and my shirt reeked of evaporating rain as I hurriedly peeled it off. As I pulled my shirt over my head, an image of the warden behind his desk, smiling and rubbing his hands together in victory, popped into my head. The thought was so ridiculous I had to grin at myself. After showering and putting on dry state whites, I made a warm cup of coffee and sat in the TV area.

During this time of day, the cell block was quieter than usual since most inmates were glued to the television, watching the daily run of soap operas. Even hardened convicts tried to catch every episode. Usually, there was chaos over what to watch, so we had to vote daily. But as many times as I had watched TV in prison, I had yet to see a vote for soap operas. No one opposed them, and if they did, a bloodshed stabbing might have occurred—that's how serious they were about their soaps.

Ten minutes was all I could stand. Every time a scene reached its high point, a striking chord of music played before flashing to another scene. I couldn't watch a show that kept me in suspended awe for weeks, trying to find out what happened to Joe Blow.

I awoke Monday morning feeling sprightly. When the sergeant's voice boomed over the intercom for farmers to check out, I pitied those still stuck on the farm. Distressed expressions lined their faces as they exited for another tormented week of legal slavery. Some still wore the filthy clothes from Friday, unwashed and reeking. After the farmers checked out, the sergeant called for G.E.D. checkout.

A stiff breeze hit my face as I entered the G.E.D. building. Thousands of books lined the walls, with an entire set of encyclopedias shelved separately, giving them an air of importance. The instructor sat behind a wood-paneled desk, chatting on the phone. He waved me toward a cheaply built desk and held up one finger, signaling he'd be with me shortly.

Men poured in noisily, talking about the weekend like they had gone to a nightclub. Five minutes later, the program's inmate runner strolled over to me. He walked with the gait of someone who had done a lot of time, wavering side to side as if the weight of prison had altered his knees. Smiling foolishly, he placed two sheets of paper, a scantron, and a test booklet in front of me. After giving instructions, he darted away.

The test was high school level, and I breezed through it in about an hour. As the runner graded my test, I noticed he didn't use an answer sheet.

"Excuse me, but don't you need the answers to grade my test properly?"

He grinned. "Youngster, I been doing dis here for twelve years. I memorized dis whole answer form better than my own social security number."

Minutes later, he shouted, "Damn, youngsta, you aced this! The instructor gonna love having you here."

And just like that, I was a math tutor.

As the searing summer waned, the days grew longer and the nights much shorter. It seemed like no sooner had I laid my head down, the first-shift officer would be clocking in, banging rigorously on the racks with keys, broomsticks, and anything else they could find to be nerve-wracking. My first summer in prison was quickly becoming torturous.

Gladiator school was not an appropriate name for the prison during the winter, but it sure as hell was the perfect name for the summer. Heat, hostile men, and blundering authorities were mainly the cause of how Draper gained its reputation. Gangs constantly fought over power, and the farmers fought simply because they could. Those who were weak, both physically and mentally, huddled under the officers and kept their mouths shut about the daily events. Men transferred to Draper during the summer held more fear in their eyes than those transferred during the winter. Some were so frightened that the convicts who had bided a lot of time could actually smell the fear seeping from their pores.

As the new arrivals entered the camp, the convicts would stand behind the fence, staring the tenderfoots down like scavenged vultures. These men were sexual psychopaths who scouted greedily for the weakest link, always ready to pilfer an anus as soon as their game succeeded. They often plotted together in swarming groups to scare the tenderfoots into giving up their anus willingly in return for protection.

Outside of prison walls, there are thousands upon thousands of rumors about men getting raped in prison. People who have never been to prison have gruesome images in their minds about how these rapes go down. They mostly think of three or four muscular giants who wait until the deepest swell of the night before dragging a fragile victim to the bathroom, where they rotate turns holding him down, violating him as their turns come around.

I also thought like that before coming to prison. In actuality, only a few men get raped. Most are just embarrassed to tell their loved ones the truth, so the stories get fabricated infamously throughout the penal system. To be honest, a lot of these men already have homosexual tendencies when they come to prison, and a seasoned ass bandit can spot them from a mile away. They have developed a highly successful system called "putting down the boo game" to gain sex from the weakened tenderfoots.

The ass bandits would send over the largest man in the clique or the slickest talker among them to intimidate the victim. After laying down a good two-minute scare tactic, they would send two more men over to pretend as if they were saving him. The two men would then take the victim to the back of the dorm and deliver a well-rehearsed speech. It would go something like this:

"Hey man, later on that goon is gonna come back with a knife and his crew, and they gonna try to kill ya if you don't do what they say. But you can pay me and my partner here to protect ya, and ain't nobody in this whole prison gonna fuck with ya. They know how we roll in this muthafucka."

Most of the time, the victim agrees, not knowing that payment is in sexual favors. Some men catch protective custody, but the harsh lockdown conditions make them change their minds almost within the first 24 hours. Then they have to come back out to face the wolves or link in.

Those who choose to lay down with the rules fall in sync within a week or so. They go from victim to prison prostitute with power and clout, able to get any favors they want from all the men who indulge in the game. Some of the not-so-jealous veterans show them how to make tight-fitting pants, thongs, Daisy Dukes, and weekend fishnet stockings out of laundry bags—whatever they need for ultimate enticement. They also teach them how to arch their eyebrows and what to use for lipstick and fingernail polish. The bravest ones go through cruel tongue ring piercings, often in unsanitary conditions.

The "incarcerated sister" program is what they call it.

If the new inductee is feminine enough with soft features, they indoctrinate them into the clique and show them how to fatten their books and prepaid cards, both inside and outside the prison. All the wealthy guys who indulge send large amounts of cash to their cards to buy them for days or weeks at a time from the prison pimps. Prostitution was a full-on profit within the walls, just as much as it was on the gritty streets of New York.

Chapter Nine

Around the middle of July, the summer blaze soared well into heatstroke conditions. The farmers continued to check out as long as the heat did not reach ninety-eight degrees before checkout time. Hardly a day went by that I did not pray to the Lord to get me off the farm. Every evening, when the farmers checked back in, they would gripe and complain about not checking out the following day. Most farmers cited the conditions as cruel and unjust. They would come in drenched with perspiration, smelling every bit the role of a pig farmer. Their clothes would be filthy black, and their skin tones a couple of leathery shades darker.

Lumps and rashes from mosquito bites were constantly visible on the flesh of the farmers because they worked around swampy woods, breeding grounds for mosquitoes. On some of the most sweltering days, when the sergeant squealed loudly over the intercom, the farmers would gather out in the hallways, bucking the farm and its slavish conditions. The ploy would work for several minutes until over half of the officers in the camp came charging into the hallways with black gloves on their hands and battering sticks raised for those who continued to protest. They bore rugged facial expressions wicked enough to scare the devil himself.

The officers would holler at the top of their lungs for the farmers to exit the building. The intimidation always worked, especially after witnessing one or two heads get cracked wide open. I once overheard the warden say that as long as the farmers allowed this treatment to go on, the more they would be subjected to these conditions. It was almost like an experiment to them.

At the turn of August, the stifling heat had become unbearable. The farmers began resorting to painful tactics to escape the harshness of the farm. A few men banged their big toe against solid objects such as iron railings, TV benches, and even the paint-peeled cement walls. They would then submit a request form to the sick call box, citing a throbbing pain in their big toe as the ailment. At six a.m. the following morning, they would be escorted to the healthcare unit, always returning with their toenails pulled and a few weeks' stop-up from the farm. These free requests were put in so often that they started charging three dollars per visit to the healthcare unit, but it was well worth it because they were able to dodge the roasting sun long enough for the lower fall temperatures to kick in.

As the summer wore on, the tactics to dodge the farm escalated to highly painful procedures. While some farmers resorted to having their toenails pulled, others took deception matters a step further. While out in the fields, a conniving pair of men would wait vigilantly for the farm boss to avert his attention elsewhere, such as conversing with another farm boss. One of the men would strike his partner on the leg with the back of the iron-welded hoe. The arc of the swing was supposed to be at an angled blow, with just the right amount of pressure a little above the ankle.

If executed properly, the ankle would swell to resemble a bad sprain. By the time the farm boss turned his head, the injured guy would be rolling on the ground, moaning miserably about twisting his ankle. Sometimes, too much force was applied to the swing, and the ankle snapped in two, resembling the sharp crackle of sun-dried twigs. The injured guy would be hauled away to the healthcare unit, where he would receive a summer-long stop-up from the farm and all other inside work duties. I cannot count on ten hands how many times I have seen farmers hobbling away from the healthcare unit on crutches. Large Kool-Aid smiles were indented across their faces as they braced the pink slip like a Willy Wonka golden ticket into the famed factory.

Judging by the furnace-like heat emanating from the cement walls in the cell blocks, one could not blame the men for taking drastic measures to escape near-death work conditions. I probably would have done something even crazier to escape the subservient conditions.

There was no relief or cool spots in the entire dorm. Every afternoon reminded me of the voyage of slaves' book that I once read, where it described the cramped and clammy fatal conditions the slaves were forced to endure, where many died and were tossed overboard like trash. The treatment was quite different, but the overcrowding factors were similar in nature.

Over two hundred bunk beds were stuffed into a dorm that was built to hold a hundred bunks at full capacity. At night, when the yards and hallways were locked down, the body heat from three to four hundred steamy, sweat-glazed males only added to the suffrage. About eighty percent of the men walked around almost completely naked, fanning themselves with cardboard-made fans and paperback books. No socks, shoes, or pants were worn—just shower slides and two pairs of boxers to block the goods from ass bandits. Some men waited until the officers made their rounds and snuck into the shower to take cold wash-offs at the risk of a beatdown for running water after the showers were supposed to be on lockdown.

Two ancient-looking fans were placed behind the two sets of stairs that led to the second tier. The motors were so old and overly used that they barely had enough power to rotate the large fans, which were our only source of relief on each tier. Because the fans were so weak, the breeze only traveled a short distance. Therefore, half-naked men crowded the entire length of the steps, sapping whatever relief the dorm would be getting had the steps remained clear.

Cold showers were a relief, but we only had four hours of access to them throughout the entire day. Some men stayed in the showers for hours because they were not monitored during the allotted time. So, some men went without showers on some days. The farmers and hall runners were allowed a shower right after check-in from the farm to help ease overcrowding during nightly shower times. I avoided the usage of lotion after showers because the stifling heat extracted lotion and oil from the skin faster than machine-pumped oil wells.

Day in and day out, the cement walls and floors sweated constantly. I never knew cement sweated before I had to suffer my time in the cement kilns. Condensation beaded up like transparent pimples on the walls, and the floors stayed grimy from the combination of dirt on the soles of shoes mixing with the slick moistness of the floor. It was fair to say the days were the hottest, but the nights were far more fretful, especially on the days when the custody farm squad mowed the yard, decimating ant beds and sending flying ants swarming angrily. Fat mosquitoes lived amongst the growing grass, and they, too, flew about annoyingly. They would exact their revenge in the wee hours of the night.

To help with the extraction of heat in the cellblock, every window remained locked in the up position. Swarms of flying ants, mosquitoes, and gnats flew noisily through the windows, particularly attracted to the illustrious glow that beamed from the many sets of fluorescent bulbs that pumped in heat like a dryer. The gnats were the worst. They flew in whirlwind formation, swarming all over the dorm, resembling an insect twister.

Homemade flyswatters proved to be formidable weapons when battling the insects, but we could not stay up all night killing them. This is when they attacked ferociously. Angry ants balled up in tiny coils and stung the skin, while greedy mosquitoes filled their tiny sacks with our fresh blood. On several occasions, I fell victim to the insects' wrath, waking up in the morning to reddish swells and itchy spots on my arm and neck that could not be appeased.

★★★

Without a doubt, the blistering summer months issued far more than their share of torture, but the increased yard time was well appreciated. Every evening, I was afforded an extra hour or two on the weight pile, grinding excessively to work off the weight I had gained during the winter. Men who had bided time for several years flaunted around the iron pile with their shirts off, sinewy, ripped muscles decorating every patch of skin above the waist as though they were warming up to pose for *Muscle & Fitness* magazine. Silly smirks and sideways glances delivered silent messages to the newer faces, as if to say—*If you want to get a workout on this pile, you need to see me, the paid-for trainer.*

For some reason, the biggest men believed they owned the weight pile. True, they were on the weight team and had won trophies for the institutional sports department, but that did not give them exclusive rights to the weights. Even the officers were brainwashed into this crazy mode of thinking. They carried around a list of the weight team members and, every day, no matter the circumstances or weather, they allowed only those men to enter the yard first. The rest of us were locked out while the weight team lifted all the iron they wanted. By the time we newcomers were allowed in, the exhausted gorillas had all the weights stacked up, which meant the iron still belonged to them—so do not touch anything stacked. We were relegated to a few big plates, several small weights, and some dumbbells.

Some men fell for this old-school penitentiary game, eventually paying these ignorant muscle heads coffee and cigarettes just to lift weights. If they had any sense, they would have known the weights belonged to the state and nowhere did it say a man had to pay for iron. I quickly noticed that only the frail cowards who were too afraid to speak out against the injustice paid up.

Most of the men who lifted weights all day long did so mainly for intimidation purposes. Beneath all those muscles lay the heartless stick men they truly were. I had seen men who didn't weigh 160 pounds soaking wet slam and pound these muscle freaks into worthless heaps within minutes. Their overly tight muscles restricted them in combat. I learned instantly that muscles in prison meant nothing—just a quicker means for the intimidated man to grab his blade instead of using his hands.

After two or three tedious hours on the weight pile, I would shoot a game or two of basketball to loosen my tightened muscles. Nearing the end of August, I took weightlifting completely out of my daily schedule so I could play in the basketball league. That didn't last long, though, because nearly every game erupted into a riot among the losing teams. Bleachers and dry-rotted benches were dragged courtside for spectators—instigators, really. They yelled all sorts of obscenities, and some even threw small rocks to help their homeboys seal victories against better teams.

Besides basketball, there were softball, horseshoes, and volleyball tournaments. Races were also held to determine who was the fastest man in the camp. Outside of prison, no one enjoyed sports more than the ones playing them. Inside, though, no one enjoyed the games like the *sista hood*. They wore their shortest shorts and flimsy headbands all summer long, cheerleading on the sidelines to give their undercover men that extra boost to pull off a win. It was hilarious because the *sista hood* performed cheering routines similar to urban high school cheerleaders. They chanted and raved excitedly while managing difficult splits and backflips to complete their routine. On the football field, they huddled tight and tossed one of their sisters fifteen feet in the air with sheer masculine strength.

It was always easy to tell who they were cheering for. Players who had been slacking on the court would suddenly speed up their game, tighten their defense, and display an arrogant hustle when handling the ball. The undercover boyfriends were so lost in elation that they didn't even notice the snickering laughter and sarcastic comments from their teammates.

Volleyball and softball tournaments were even wilder. The prison women had their own softball team, which got devoured every time they played. Game-ending scores resembled basketball scores, while the *sista hood* scored fewer points than a little league soccer game. It didn't matter how badly they were losing; they still cheered as if they had the highest score. Volleyball, though, belonged to them. All the white prison women lay half-naked on their towels, tanning themselves while watching their sisters play. It was easy to get jealous of how much fun they always seemed to have. They woke up every day as if they were in a fantasy land, while the rest of us barely clung to our sanity, focusing on gaining our freedom as quickly as possible.

It was obvious why they were always in festive moods. They had a constant eyeful of muscular men, especially around the shower area. On top of that, they practically ran the prison. Most of the drugs in prison were made readily available because of them. They smuggled them in through gruesome methods that didn't bother them in the least. Some literally damaged their insides, shoving drug-wrapped packages the size of rifle barrels up their rectums. The smartest ones worked in spots where drugs could be brought to them for an excessive fee.

All the best jobs in the camp were assigned to the prison women. They had a network with the female officers, who enjoyed their company while at work. Rarely was a prison woman assigned to the farm squad. The laundry room, law library, administration aid, and program aide jobs were the hardest to get because the *sista hood* had those positions locked down. There was no dodging their network if you were into the legal side of things.

If a man wanted new clothes and boots before his six-month renewal, he had to go through their network. If he wanted to jump the list for a program that could lead to parole cuts, he had to strike a deal with a sister. Otherwise, he had to wait his turn.

Over half the camp was run by female officers, and they always sided with their workers. They would open cell blocks to allow a sister from another dorm in to perform sexual acts for money. But if a straight man was caught masturbating to an illegal porn magazine, he would be written up, put on 45-day restriction from phone calls, visits, and store draws, and thrown in lock-up for the same amount of time.

Many nights, I lay on my rack pondering the system's motive. Rehabilitation was long forgotten. Education, reform, job skill courses, and addiction programs were practically dismantled. The entire system was mapped for maximum violence. Hundreds of violent men were piled into a single dorm with just one or two officers. There was no way two men could stop gambling, fights, sexual romps, and stabbings while also monitoring the front door to keep outsiders from attacking their enemies. It was too much. So, many inmates took advantage of the chaos, controlling and profiting off sex. Inside these walls, sex was more of an industry than drugs.

Men played roles like actors—thugs and gangsters by day, closet queens by night. They started by screwing the sisters, then fell madly in love. The sisters got bored and threatened to leave, so the men offered themselves to keep the relationship going. Many sisters bragged about turning hardcore thugs out, just as Cleopatra seduced Julius Caesar to promote her culture's dominance despite being ruled by Greece.

It followed a pattern. First, they snuck around. Then, they stopped caring who found out. Love turned to violence, extreme jealousy, and a willingness to kill or maim anyone who interfered. Some men starved themselves to feed their sisters, only to rack up debts, get locked up for fighting, and lose their woman within an hour to the next big spender.

★★★

As August ended and September rolled in, the sun's heat grew even more intense. My skin had undergone a complete transformation, darkening from a shaded brown to the color of deep wood. The only upside to the heat was the weight I sweated off my midsection.

Fights and box break-ins continued to plague the dorm, and with nothing better to do, men started bringing in insects, frogs, lizards, and even small snakes as pets. It was against the rules to sneak in bugs and other pests, but inside the prison walls, rules were rarely followed.

Snakes, field mice, lizards, frogs, spiders, and beetles flooded the dorms because inmates were willing to trade packs of cigarettes and bags of coffee for new pets. Most were smuggled in by farmers during weak shakedowns. Men walked around the camp with green frogs and lizards clinging to their shirts like snails withering along cement walls.

Some of the more depraved inmates captured animals and insects for profit, tying strings around their bodies and betting on which one would topple the other. Nearly everything became a business opportunity. The pet trade became so serious that it caused broken friendships. On checkout days, pet owners had to find someone to watch their animals while they were away. Some men treated their pets like children or best friends from the free world, demanding the same level of care. Harming or neglecting a pet was no different than committing an offense against another inmate.

If a pet died under a sitter's watch, violent fights and even stabbings followed, especially over kittens, snakes, and rabbits. These were the hardest to sneak in but, once inside, were nurtured like infants. Most were kept outside in the yard and fed daily, but at night, they were often hidden in property boxes.

Not everyone cared about animal life. Some killed snakes on the farm, brought them inside, and skinned them. They bought salt balls from kitchen workers to cure the hides, which they then sold to the guys in the leather workshop. The workshop produced snakeskin belts and purses, selling them to inmates, officers, and visitors for a profit. Rabbits were caught but rarely kept alive for long. They were skinned, cleaned, and cooked in the microwave with seasonings bought from kitchen workers, or handed over with a pack of cigarettes to be cooked in the chow hall.

Like I said earlier, nearly every aspect of human interaction inside the prison was monetized. Skills from the outside were put to use for survival when money from loved ones dried up. Some men used their talents, while others resorted to selling their bodies—either way, it was about survival.

As more animals poured in, so did diseases. Spider bites became rampant, pubic and hair lice spread as men slept, and rats invaded property boxes, nibbling on snacks. The most feared was the infamous brown recluse spider. A single bite could leave a hole the size of a quarter, burrowing deep enough that doctors had to dig clear to the bone to remove the infection.

Staph infections, tuberculosis, hepatitis, HIV, and syphilis were among the deadliest diseases. The prison took extreme measures to prevent outbreaks since these illnesses could spread like wildfire. Twice a year, every inmate had to undergo physicals and bloodwork. If a disease was detected, the infected inmate was sent to lock-up or the infirmary for treatment. Tuberculosis and HIV cases were transferred to Kilby immediately. When an outbreak occurred, the entire camp went on lockdown—no one in, no one out—until everyone was retested.

Inmates infected with sexually transmitted diseases were required to list every sexual partner they had. If they refused, the prison imposed quarantine measures. Those who cooperated often turned in lists with dozens of names. Occasionally, officers' names appeared. Temptation didn't discriminate against blue uniforms.

Rumors spread fast, the biggest one being about a white Sisterhood member who allegedly turned in a list of seventy-one names. Shocking? Not really. Many black men sought out white Sisterhood members, and it was common to see an eight-man procession sneaking into the bathroom for sex with one.

As rumors flew, men who crept around at night walked the halls sluggishly, wide-eyed with worry. Their sunken faces resembled the cursed character from Stephen King's *Thinner*.

Of all diseases, hepatitis and staph were the most common. Hepatitis spread mainly among inmates who injected drugs. Syringes were rare, so needles were shared without concern. Tattoos also contributed to hepatitis outbreaks. Prison tattoo artists used makeshift needles, often filed-down paper clips. Attempts to sterilize them involved bleaching and burning the tips, but this step was usually only taken when the client insisted.

The careless ones who rushed to get tattoos without checking hygiene often paid the price. Dirty needles and filth turned the prison into a breeding ground for staph infections. With conditions similar to an unclean nursing home, avoiding staph was nearly impossible. Those lucky enough to dodge hepatitis still ended up covered in grotesque, spongy lumps—the costly effects of staph.

If an inmate's infection was traced back to a tattoo, he'd receive a major disciplinary charge: forty-five days in lock-up and farm duty. He'd also lose visits, phone calls, and store privileges for the same period. To avoid punishment, infected inmates avoided the health unit and tried to treat themselves. They waited until the sore grew to the size of a half-dollar, then spent minutes—sometimes hours—squeezing the slimy core out of a hole no bigger than a pencil head.

The core often burrowed deep, requiring a homeboy to help extract it. What came out resembled oversized kidney stones drenched in spit-up phlegm. If they failed to remove the entire core and the long trailing tail that followed, the infection would return. Many times, they lost their grip, and the core would slip back in, as if magnetized to bone.

Even from a distance, the sight of the core's exposure was enough to make a lion regurgitate its dinner. It left a hole so deep it looked like acid had been poured on the skin. Sometimes, the infection burrowed all the way to the bone. Once the core was removed, the wound would slowly begin to heal, leaving behind a hard, blackened scar.

This should have been the end of the infection, but careless men let the bacteria spread—leaking onto sinks, toilets, blankets, and common areas like the TV room. When inmates went to the health unit with staph, nurses lied, calling it a spider bite to avoid scrutiny from families and health inspectors. Yet, they still administered daily antibiotic injections.

The cover-up worked until officers started contracting staph. Then, the warden quarantined the prison. No transfers in, no transfers out. The epidemic had to be controlled.

By sheer luck and extreme caution, I made it through the pandemic unscathed.

Chapter Ten

As my first hellish summer ended, I felt well adapted enough that nothing could break me. September rolled around without much relief. It was not as hot as July and August, but in Alabama, temperatures in excess of seventy-five and eighty degrees were normal. My daily routine kept me busy enough to stay away from illegal activities, and I was making excellent progress at school. Four of my students obtained their G.E.D., and two more were taking the practice test.

Everything was going smoothly for me until I was thrown in segregation for fighting. Every year, men who were released from segregation returned to the population ten to fifteen pounds lighter. Their skin complexion would be so pale it appeared to have been bleached. This was due to a lack of sunlight from being cooped up in the darkened cement sweatbox. Men who harbored the most savage attitudes were easily broken by the harsh treatment that occurred in segregation. Inhumane stories about the agonizing conditions were more than enough to keep me in compliance with the rules. I managed to keep my quick-to-smart-off tongue in check, especially when dealing with officers who thought all inmates were cattle heading to the slaughterhouse. I made a silent vow to stay within the guidelines so that I would never have to experience segregation's torture.

Sadly, though, this vow was broken. I had managed to contain my tongue and smart-aleck comments for so long that the suppressed tension was like a terrorist's rage against a spoiled American infidel. I never noticed how dangerous my pent-up anger had become until the altercation at the microwave.

It was a long, hot September evening when meat patties were being served for dinner. I decided to eat a sandwich from the canteen rather than stare longingly at the burnt, greenish-brown chow hall patty. While returning to the cell to heat up the sandwich, I saw a long line at the downstairs microwave. It was obvious that most men in the cell had also decided to skip out on the chow hall dinner.

I was super hungry and impatient, so I walked to the upstairs microwave. Surprisingly, there was only one man there—or more like one big, beefy convict. There was no question in my mind why the microwave was without a long wait line after seeing who the guy was. This guy was a brutal bully who intimidated a lot of young, first-time offenders with his fifteen-year convict status. He was standing at the microwave with his shirt off, holding two cups of water and watching something else heat up. There was enough hair on his back to make me think twice about the evolution theory that man evolved from apes.

My first instinct was to turn around, but hunger and the thought of him hogging the microwave urged me on. I stood behind him for several minutes, staring at the gross, melted-looking bumps at the base of his neck. By the time he pulled his first cup of water out of the microwave, the sergeant began yelling over the intercom for all inmates to report to their assigned racks for institutional count.

Anger trickled through every bone in my body. This rude ape was purposely hogging the oven because he felt like he had institutional privilege. Even though I was angry, I still asked him in a calm voice if I could please use the oven for a quick minute before count time. Count time usually took about twenty minutes—double that for a recount. A minute was all I asked for so I could run downstairs and enjoy my double cheeseburger during count time.

He reacted as I expected him to. His eyes were colder than the Ice Age as he turned swiftly to face me. A stiff frown ran down the length of his fat face as if I had asked him a life-or-death question. I instinctively stepped back from his contorted face. Before I could say, "Forget about it," he began shouting and screaming at me like I was a kid, putting on a show for the dorm. As he screamed, his lips drew back on his teeth in a menacing snarl, mimicking a rabid alpha wolf attacking an innocent child.

I must say, his size and anger intimidated me—but that's where he went wrong. Whenever I became fearful, a rush of adrenaline would churn through my muscles, increasing my reaction time and strength tremendously. Literally, I could feel my body prickle in a state of intense arousal. My heart began pounding loud enough for me to hear it echo in my head, and my blood pressure shot up so high I thought my cranium would explode.

I guess he figured he had me scared enough to piss my pants because he stepped close enough to stand on top of my toes. The fetid onion smell on his breath was so pungent a skunk would have tucked its tail and run. After summing up his speech, he finished off with some words brutal enough to make me want to kill him.

"Nigga, you sleep downstairs, so you ain't gonna use this mufucka till I get through wit it, country boy. Clown-ass nigga tryna rush me like you some kinda gator."

He stood hulking over me for another second or two, then walked to his rack to put up his first cup of steaming hot water. I wanted to turn around, but my pride wouldn't let me face all those piercing stares already clawing through my back. Maybe I was being paranoid at the moment, but I sensed the ass bandits staring hard enough to burn right through to my soul.

Something had to be done, or I was going to receive a hell of a lot of late-night sexual offers. Without looking behind me, I walked nonchalantly to the microwave, pulled out his second cup of hot water, and waited for the ape to run up yapping. He jumped up immediately and began power-walking toward me. As soon as he got within five feet—fuming with a cold, hard stare and blood boiling mad—I dashed the heated water in his face.

All the hot water didn't reach the intended mark, but enough of it singed the ape's face to make him stumble backward, cupping his pudgy hands to his heated skin. The second he brought his hands down, I began throwing solidly structured blows. The first punch landed square on his chin.

Those once frosted eyes quickly became white marbles rolling around in his hoggish-sized head. Before he crumbled, I landed a stiff haymaker into the tender flesh under his right eye. I could feel my knuckles shift a bit as the blow reverberated with a smacking sensation. And it hurt like hell. I was relieved to see the ape timber like a severed pine tree because a third blow would have done major damage to my fist. When he collided with the cement floor, his stomach jiggled like cold jelly.

I didn't stop there because I'd seen enough fights in prison to know you had to inflict major damage when fighting or quit sleeping at night. Sleeping in a dorm that housed three hundred inmates made it easy for an enemy to creep up on you in the dark. It was imperative for me to strike fear in the ape's heart to keep him from retaliating.

Before his sagging gut ceased wobbling, my legs were doing the A-Town Stomp dance across his face and ribs. He balled up like a shelled turtle and started yelling he was good, which in prison meant he was done. But I was not. I tried to kick him in the back of his head, but he had his hands and arms wrapped around his skull.

I heard heavy boots thudding across the floor and looked up just in time to see the quick-moving procession of blue cloth appearing in my left vision. Without hesitation, I stepped back from the wailing ape and flung my arms toward the ceiling. I didn't offer resistance. Two of the husky officers exhaled an angry puff of air when they saw me cooperate. They were surely intent and primed on getting in some batting practice.

I was handcuffed and shoved roughly to the shift office. The shift sergeant questioned me about the events that led to the fight, nodding and frowning as the story progressed. When I finished telling the story, the sergeant told me that had I not used hot water, I could have signed a living agreement and dodged lock-up.

Upon hearing my name and "segregation unit" mentioned in the same conversation, I slumped down in my seat and tried to explain my way out. It wasn't working, so I shut my mouth and accepted the punishment.

I was escorted to the end of the hall, where the door leading to segregation was located. A rush of heated air whooshed through the entrance as soon as the door was opened. With the heat came the disgusting smell of musty, sweaty flesh. We continued through a long, narrow corridor that led to the single-man cells.

Upon sight of the small unit, my jaw sagged like a drooling child. Nervous beads of sweat trickled down my forehead and into the slits of my eyes. Because my hands were restrained, the salty sweat agitated my eyes with the burning vigor of mace.

The officer noticed me squirming and smiled twistedly. "Welcome to the Mexican jail," he mouthed in an eerie voice.

I was about to mouth off smartly until a metallic clicking on the back wall interrupted my thoughts. Upon closer inspection, I noticed an inmate handcuffed to the wall. His perplexed expression was glazed over with perspiration. From my perspective, the paunchy guy looked exhausted from standing for hours, his knees bent slightly to relieve the pressure off his heels. He stared at me with weeping eyes until the officer nudged me inside the cell.

BANG! The officer slammed the thick metal door so quick and hard that the echo sounded like Operation Desert Storm during a bomb raid. With plenty of gruff anger in his voice, the officer ordered me to stick my hands through the small slit in the door to have my handcuffs removed.

The sweatbox was much smaller than I had perceived, and instead of one bunk, there were two. A single, heavily barred window that couldn't be opened was cut into the upper portion of the wall. It was pocked with several marble-sized holes, the reason for which I learned the following day. Besides the rusted bunks, the only other furnishings were a corroded sink, heavily littered with dry specks of toothpaste.

My half-naked bunkmate, whose skin was pallid brown from being deprived of sunlight, sat up on his rack with a cheesy grin on his face. Without even a simple greeting, he began drilling me with questions about what I had done and what was happening in the world (the prison world). I couldn't blame him. After several long days of being alone, even the walls quit talking.

"Whatcha in fa?"

"Fighting."

"What about you?"

"Oh, dey say I stabbed someone."

"They say? Is it true?"

"Yea and den no." *(For reasons not to incriminate himself, since he still had to go to trial, and a guilty plea could result in him getting fifteen more years.)*

We continued talking—me about the prison happenings, and him lacing me up about the heat and other rugged obstacles in lock-up. After an hour or so, the heat dancing off the stone walls became stifling, elevating the raunchy smells of mildew, sweat, and musk to toxic levels of pure disgust. I walked over to the sink to splash cool water on my face but turned away after seeing its contents. The faucet hummed a little before spurting out foggy water. I became infuriated, wondering how in the hell I was going to survive time in Lil' Mexico.

Around six a.m. the following morning, I was awakened by the noisy jingling of keys turning in the door lock. Before I could wipe the crud from my eyes, two segregation officers stepped into the cell.

"Alright, you musty muthafuckas, get outta dem beds."

"For what?" I angrily asked.

"Because we takin' dem mats, that's for what. Now, is dat gonna be a problem? 'Cause you act like you wanna buck the system."

I thought about the rumors I had heard about segregation officers beating inmates over the head with socks stuffed with bars of soap. I quickly jumped out of bed and dragged my mat off it and into the hall.

Around seven a.m., I was given a white jumpsuit so I could be taken outside for the required one-hour recreation time. The entire segregation unit was taken to a small fenced-in area identical to Kilby's East Dorm gated yard. Everyone was handcuffed to prevent any fighting since the inmates we had altercations with were also present. As we were being led back to the sweatboxes, I took one long look at the sun because it was my new enemy. The one fate I did know—this was one battle I wasn't going to win.

Back in the sweatbox, the heat was already blaring from the cement walls. I immediately stripped down to my two pairs of boxers and listened to my headphones, trying to take my mind off the heat. I was thankful to be on the green level, which meant I was pending investigation. On a green card, a segregation inmate was still allowed to use their radio. Once an inmate was found guilty, he got switched from green level to pink.

Pink level was when the weight loss came into play. All snack items were removed from the property box. No radios were allowed, and only two meals a day were served.

I alternated between lying on the bare iron rack and pacing the steam room to relieve the cramps in my back. It felt like I had walked a million circles, yet lunch had yet to roll around. The timing process had already become agonizing, moving at the speed of a nervous snail.

As hunger pains knocked against the walls of my stomach, a raucous rumbling of metal and squeaking wheels echoed through the segregation hallway. Like a symphony cued by a director, the unit swiftly became a live concert. Brazen voices from the end of the hallway rang out as starved inmates crowded the small slits in their doors. Even my bunkmate was huddled around the door slit, waiting impatiently to see which inmate was pushing the food cart. Not only was he hoping, but I was silently praying the runner was someone I knew. In these ravaging conditions, an extra helping was highly warranted.

My hopes soared when I spotted my neighbor from three cells down serving the trays—only to be crushed just as quickly when he turned me down for extras. Instead of being the tough guy he had portrayed in population, my old neighbor was acting like a field slave, keeping a watchful eye for potential escapees. His voice trembled as he denied my request.

"I... I... I can't be givin' dese folks stuff out like dis. If I get caught, dey gone chunk me right back on da farm, and I ain't goin' dere for nobody."

I understood his side of the story later, but at that moment, my growling stomach didn't give a damn about his fear. I wanted to snatch him straight through the slit and stomp my foot down his throat. Sensing my anger, he slid my tray through the opening and hurriedly moved on to the next unit.

Hunger completely blocked out the repulsion I had for the meat patty when I was in population. I took one look at the charred meat and shriveled vegetables before devouring the meal like it was a delicacy. Everything was cold, especially the vegetables. They tasted like they had been poured straight out of the can. The food was so cold it slid down my throat in slow, thick clumps. I had to chase it down with the bitter, sour drink they served in a Styrofoam cup not even big enough for a kid's tea party.

Ten minutes after wolfing down the food, a sour aftertaste lingered in the back of my throat. It made me sick to my stomach. The stale toothpaste barely put a dent in changing the topsy-turvy taste, so I laid down and forced myself to sleep.

After what seemed like hours, Mr. Heat slapped me awake with vigor. Dewy sweat taped my face to the iron rack, making a Velcro-like sound as I peeled myself away from the warm bunk. On top of that, the hair under my arms had absorbed so much moisture that every movement felt like pressing soaked sponges against my sides.

A barefooted thudding came from by the door. As soon as I turned my head, I saw my half-naked cellmate doing jumping jacks.

How big of an idiot can one be? I asked myself before exploding with a heat-flared temper.

"Hey man, is you gone fucking crazy or what?"

"Naw, partna, I'm just tryna stay in shape so I can bust dat weight pile up on dem clowns out dere. I know dey ready fa me to fall off."

"Man, we 'bout to suffocate in dis small-ass room with no circulation, and yo dumb ass over dere puttin' out nothin' but heat and funk. You smell like a boxing gym, and I ain't about to lay up in heah smellin' yo stank ass, bruh."

He looked at me with little understanding before agreeing to just one more set of push-ups before calling it quits for the day.

I told him I'd appreciate it and then asked about shower time since we were already on the subject of funk.

"Oh, we took showers yesterday before you came in, so it'll be another day before you get yours."

"Another day?" I blurted out. "Shit, I'm gettin' musty just sittin' here, and you over there puttin' out like a pair of week-worn socks. So what we supposed to do about that besides get headaches from sniffin' funk and must all day?"

He told me he had been in segregation for twelve days and had gotten used to it. Complaining, like I was doing now, wasn't helping. If I wanted to survive, I had to focus on staying cool rather than whining.

He was right about that.

I walked over to the fountain, ran the cold water, and rinsed off as best as I could. The moment I cut the water off, my forehead beaded right back up with sweat. This was pointless. All I could do was sit down and meditate with as little movement as possible.

While I meditated, my cellmate got busy working on some kind of contraption. It was a tightly rolled piece of paper, held together by a string tied around the middle. One end of the rolled paper had a small opening, while an extremely long string was securely tied to the other. As he worked feverishly, my curiosity got the best of me.

"What in the hell you riggin' up?"

His reply was comical to me at the time.

"I'm makin' a fishin' pole so I can go fishin' at yard call."

I laughed until my stomach muscles ached. For a moment, I thought his days alone had driven him to extreme delirium.

"What lake you fishin' in?" I asked, smirking.

He shot me a "Shut the fuck up sometimes" look.

"Watch and learn," he whispered.

He glanced up toward the high window, then carefully guided the paper pole through a small hole. Inside the pole was a note along with three stamps—payment for a few hand-rolled Bugler cigarettes.

From the yard, we could hear inmates arguing over who had next on the basketball court. My cellmate's eyes lit up like two hundred-watt bulbs. He started fiendishly jerking the string up and down, trying to make it noticeable to anyone nearby. I pictured the pole dancing in the air like a shiny lure attracting a wide-mouthed bass.

Minutes ticked by before his expression darkened with nervousness.

"What's the matter, man? You lookin' like the world 'bout to end," I said.

"Dis here da tricky part. Sometimes a pie-ass thief come by and steal my lil' stamps and shit. Dey ain't got no respect for da game 'cause dey ain't never been through dis lock-up shit. And den, you got other problems. Sometimes monkey-ass officers in da tower look real hard for shit like dis. They call dis in real quick if they see us fishin'. Dat's more days added to seg time."

"We in here fishing?" I blurted out, quickly correcting him. "You mean yo' ass in here fishing."

"Well, you know what I meant to say," he snapped back.

Just then, the line went taut for a few seconds before slackening again.

"Go ahead and pull dat shit up before yo' ass get caught," I said, irritated.

"Not yet," he murmured. "Dat's just somebody takin' out da stamps and note."

Two agonizing minutes passed before the string gave a sharp tug, jerking my cellmate's arm. His eyes gleamed as he pulled the pole back in. The stamps were gone. In their place were three fat, hand-rolled cigarettes and the torn half of a matchbox with six matches and the striker still attached. A satisfied grin spread across his face as he fumbled with his catch of the day.

He tore the blue wrapper off the tissue roll from our cell, its texture resembling cigarette paper, and re-rolled eight smaller cigarettes from the three fat ones.

"How in the hell do y'all come up with this shit?" I asked.

"Survival." He shrugged. "When you damn near dead in a hole, you get real creative. Da best shit, yo' best ideas, come in dis solitary hole. In a week, you gonna feel like a prophet, like you got a gift to change da world. Dis place strips all dem distractions away. Out there, you lost, chasin' everything but what's really in da heart."

I nodded, thinking hard about what he was saying. There was so much more to me than this hole. I hoped something good would come out of this—a light to guide me back to where I was supposed to be. I sat there, lost in thought, until sleep pulled me under.

A constant tapping on my shoulder startled me awake. My cellmate nudged me, telling me to grab my mat and covers.

At the mention of the mat, I bolted upright, still groggy, nearly falling flat on my face. I flung the mat onto the rack, climbed on, and slept like a baby.

I never thought I'd say this, but that night, the thin mat felt like a Sealy Posturepedic.

The next day was the weekend, which meant we got to keep our mats. Taking full advantage, I slept all day, waking only for meals and bathroom breaks.

After dinner, segregation officers made their rounds, finally granting us our long-overdue showers. Only two inmates at a time were allowed in the shower area, with barely enough time to get clean.

I soaped down twice, but before I could finish rinsing, time was up. We weren't even allowed to dry off. Instead, we had to walk back to our cells, half-naked, our boxers still wet. It was a quickie, but damn, it felt good to be clean.

The rest of the weekend passed like a fleeting thought. It was bearable—no officers yelling, no mats being taken, just a quiet, sleepy comfort that made it an ideal time to reflect on my future.

Monday came, and everything snapped back to protocol.

The only good thing about weekdays was the small commissary order I was allowed to purchase. Beyond that, it was pure hell. Each shift had its own twisted methods to maintain control over the segregation block. Remorse from a segregation officer? Unheard of.

If one unit messed up, the whole block got punished.

Talking across cells was strictly forbidden. To enforce the rule, officers resorted to the cruelest measures. If first shift heard too much noise, they issued a warning. If the talking continued, the violator got an unpleasant visit from two or three officers.

Hearing a grown man being beaten for talking was enough to make even the hardest criminals fight back tears.

Sorrowful cries would ring out, echoing through the halls like a murder victim's final plea for salvation before the death blow.

"Please don't hit me no more, please, please… Jesus! I can't take it no more. I'll stop talkin', I swear, officer!"

Sometimes, the entire segregation unit would erupt into chaos—kicking and beating on doors, screaming at the top of their lungs, throwing paper or whatever else they could squeeze through the door slits. It was a protest, a warning to the officers that the beatings wouldn't be tolerated forever. A message: keep this up, and something bad is bound to happen.

Second and third shifts operated differently from first shift. They didn't single out one unit for talking too much. Instead, they punished everyone.

When someone refused to shut up, the officers turned the heat up—especially during the day when the outside temperature was already scorching. Men bound for hell didn't have to wait for death to feel its flames. The cement-walled cells trapped enough heat to fry chicken without grease.

Most days, the sun-baked walls caused mirages to ripple across the concrete. Every possible method to cool down was exhausted. Most men stripped to their boxers and lay on the sweaty floor. When the heat from their bodies warmed the concrete, they poured water over it. Within thirty minutes, the water evaporated, and the process repeated—over and over, all day long.

Watching my cellmate go back and forth from the sink reminded me of those old country women hauling well water for a bath.

★★★

One blistering night during my second week, the block was louder than usual. The segregation officer on duty—pissed off, probably from some domestic dispute—had no patience to deal with us. Instead of the usual warning to quiet down, the heat just flicked on.

It blasted through the vents, thick with the stench of burning plastic.

Within minutes, the block was sweltering. Agonized cries echoed through the cells, like damned souls screaming from purgatory. Some men tried to act tough, cursing out the officer. Others just begged.

"Turn it off! Please, man!"

"I can't breathe in this shit!"

"It burns when I take a deep breath!"

The heat shut off—for five minutes. Then it came roaring back, even hotter. Over and over, it pulsed through the block, punishing the innocent and guilty alike.

My cellmate grabbed his cup and walked toward the sink. I figured he was about to pour water on the floor again. But instead, he dumped it on his bare mat and plopped down on it.

A sickening squish—like a thousand crushed insects—oozed from under his back.

Minutes later, he was snoring like a baby.

It looked so damn refreshing, I tried it myself.

It was a hell of a remedy—because I didn't even remember falling asleep.

Chapter Eleven

As the week trickled by, the combination of sticky sweat, dirt, and water caked up on the floor began drifting off a violently bitter smell—something like sewage water. The mops and brooms had not been brought in for over a week, and the reeking stench was performing calamitous kicks in my nostrils. Heat was still a problem, but not a major one. The more suffering my body endured, the more susceptible it became to adaptation. Push-ups became a part of my daily routine, and hunger was a thing of the past.

While still on the administration level, I was given my one phone call for the month. The sound of my mother's voice was equivalent to the victory of winning an Oscar. As she fought back tears on one end, I struggled with flooded emotions on the other. There was so much worry in her voice that I found it hard to tell her the truth about my situation, so I lied to her. It was more than enough stress to have her one and only son locked away. That pain alone was worse than having a dagger cast through the eye. I told her that I was doing great and that we received the same treatment in lock-up that we received in population. She asked how I was eating, and I told her we got fed good, hot meals three times a day. The only negative was that we were not given the opportunity to work out, I told her. The lie burned as it slithered off my tongue, but it was a relief to spare her the grief and worry about my survival.

Despite my efforts to soothe her worries, there was still sorrow in her voice.

"Well, baby, lock-up ain't like what I see in those old prison movies, is it?" she asked, as if she knew I was lying to her.

"I told you, Mom, this prison lock-up thing is a joke. I can breeze through this thing standing on top of my head."

She laughed dryly, then changed the subject, leaving me with the impression that the conversation about lock-up was just too painful for her. While discussing how good things were going at home, the officer yelled that time was up, waving his hand violently for me to hang up. She became so quiet that I could have sworn she was thinking I was going to be beaten for talking over my time. Sensing the discomfort, we said our goodbyes, which was more grievous than the initial hello, before slowly placing the phone on the receiver.

I was lucky to have received my call when I did because the following week, I was found guilty. I was transferred from pink to green. If pink level was torture, then green was pure, unearthly hell. No phone calls were allowed, all snack items and radios were taken away, and we were fed only two meals a day. Green level was the real segregation, code-named the Dog House. Just as my body had adapted to three meals a day—with the help of a few snacks—I was now being forced to subject it to even worse conditions.

I was moved to a cell further down the hall, where I was thrown into a unit with a pale-skinned skeleton. His skin was in bad need of sunlight, and his teeth seemed to have absorbed too much of it. What resembled buttery glaciers was caked heavily on his teeth. I imagined his breath smelled of rotting meat from the teeth he displayed. I made a quick promise to myself to avoid all conversations with the guy. As I unpacked, he eyed me with utter contempt. Surely, he was angry with me for disturbing his lowly solace of not bathing and masturbating at will.

To my surprise, he spoke joyously, introducing himself as Goo. *There ain't a better name for you*, I said to myself right before telling him my name. We did not talk much that first day because I cut the conversation short, horribly afraid of what stench might be lurking in his mouth. There was no lunch, so I slept until dinner. After eating, I laid right back down, forcing myself to sleep even though my body was well-rested.

I tried to develop a routine strategy to deal with eating only twice a day, which was to sleep as much as possible, only waking for meals, showers, and bathroom usage. Around noontime, a boiling hunger pain startled me out of my sleep. Since there was nothing to eat, I rushed to the sink and began swallowing handfuls of foul-tasting warm water. The first few gulps only strengthened the hunger pain, but a few handfuls later, I was feeling bloated. I walked back to my bunk, thinking all kinds of crazy thoughts. It was scary being this hungry. This was a weird hunger that made one rationalize island cannibalism. Raw deer meat could have been the appetizer of the day at this moment in time.

While daydreaming about food, a quiet rattling rustled me out of my slumber. Goo was unraveling a tissue-wrapped biscuit he had saved from breakfast. I became mesmerized, watching him with hungry, depraved eyes as he flicked a few drops of water on it to soften the stale crust. It was difficult to determine if he was teasing me or not, but the crumbs falling from his mouth were temptation enough to make me want to take the scrawny guy's biscuit. Realizing that I was thinking harshly, I laid back on my rack and urged myself to sleep before a rash decision was made.

A full hour before lunch, Mr. Remorseless Hunger bubbled around my stomach with extreme vigor. Goo must have heard my stomach growling because he looked at me with a wild-eyed expression. Once again, I tried filling myself with water, but this time the famine was just too great. The hunger returned before I could even get back to sleep. It was gaining strength over me, a wolverine clawing through my stomach. The heat only added to the torture. It made my first day in the Dog House a living hell.

By the time the noisy food cart was heard rumbling in the hallway, I was starved enough to eat the wheels off of it. As the food was passed through the slit, my stomach roared like a lion preparing for battle to maintain his pride. Thankfully, the meal was spaghetti and not meat patties. Even though the meat was made from the same gory mixture, the spaghetti sauce did a pretty good job of disguising it. Instead of consuming everything on the tray, I wrapped the two rolls in tissue paper to pacify the hunger pains that were bound to arise later. Then I dealt greedily with the meal at hand.

My stomach began moaning for food around eight that night, and I was readily prepared for it. If it was a battle to survive, it was going to be fought on both sides. I was not giving in to losing my sanity. I dribbled some water on the hardened rolls, then devoured them. I imagined them as Krispy Kreme doughnuts without icing and swallowed them with eager satisfaction. Afterward, I gulped down three handfuls of water to help expand the bread in my stomach. I felt appeased enough to sleep without the same fit as the night before.

As time progressed, so did my survival tactics. The one thing that did not support growth was my waistline, which I was more than happy to see dissipate. My boxer shorts now hung limply around my waist, and my stomach was flatter than an ironing board. The countless sets of ab work I had devotedly executed in the past weeks began showing with intense definition. I could now say those washboard abs so arrogantly displayed in magazine ads were not impossible to obtain. All it takes is a lot of starvation, which I am very proud to say I hated every minute of.

While serving time in lock-up, the only thing to surprise me was the transformation of men's minds when they were bunked up with a homosexual. Without their friends around to judge them, they were free to express their temptations with another man. Men that were banging and feared in population resorted to scavengers of men in lock-up. One week, they slandered the officer with a hail of cuss words for placing them in a cell with a homosexual, and the next week, they were madly in love, refusing to even go outside for their hour of sunlight.

The men who were cellmates with a homosexual lost even more weight than everyone else in segregation. Some resembled grotesquely thin zombies as they withered away their weight by means of excessive sex and low food consumption. This happened because every time a man ejaculates, he loses up to two thousand calories. The low food intake occurred when men gave their already limited meals away to their new "girlfriend," as they termed it.

With a little over a week left to serve on my sixty-five days in the Mexican jail, I put in a request to meet with the segregation board. The segregation board held meetings with lock-up inmates to discuss issues on their case and determine whether the individual was ready for release back into the population. Depending on how long the list was for inmates waiting to serve time in lock-up, the segregation board often considered early release for those with good behavior. Another inmate with a more serious or violent crime could make my bond.

After the meeting with the segregation board, I was told consideration for early release was a possibility. Fuming with internal anger, I was escorted out of the meeting, feeling lied to and made fun of. Luckily, I did not get rowdy because two fainting-hot days later, the officer on shift ordered me to pack up. Two minutes later, I was ready to get the hell away from the most torturous memory of my life.

I had to sign a living agreement with the ape I fought before being released. I was taken to the disciplinary cell, which is where lock-up inmates must serve an additional forty-five days. The good thing, though, was that it was in population, and we were allowed the freedom to do and go as we pleased. Phone calls, visits, and store draws were still restricted, but as long as I was away from the Mexican jail, I was okay. The disciplinary cell, better known as the hot dorm, was located up a flight of stairs and designed to hold one hundred and twenty-eight people.

Halfway up the steps, my ears tuned in to the sound of a drastic argument being waged about what city ran the prison. This was going to be a *go for what you know* dorm. While turning the key in the iron-grilled door, all noise seemed to come to an eerie halt as the men turned to see what piece of fresh meat the officer was bringing to the lion's den. Before I could get three steps into the dorm, every bloodthirsty pair of eyes in the cell was on me. I kept walking to my assigned rack while at the same time looking for familiar faces.

Some men scowled at me, and others smiled, with lustful intentions marred deeply in their grins. There were a few violent troublemakers that I was none too happy to see crowded into a corner of the dorm. These were men that were supposed to be moved out to higher-security-level prisons because of their uncultivated behaviors. Not only were they a threat to society, but a threat to prison as well. There were a few other familiar faces, but none that I would associate with. Right then and there, I made the decision to do most of my time on my rack. If there was something illegal going on, I did not want any part in it. Paying attention to my new surroundings was a must because this was an *everything goes* block. One slip, and my life could be in the hands of a deranged killer.

Around five, I decided to go ahead and take my shower. I did not want to wait any later because the shower area became *Sex in the City* as soon as the lights were out. On my way to the shower, I saw men lying in bed with each other, hugged up and giving massages like a Cambodian masseuse. There was one couple cooped up on the last rack, sucking the tongues out of each other's mouths with the happy gusto of chewing on succulent smoked pig feet. I had to say *excuse me* five times before the small huddle standing in front of the shower entrance parted to let me through. There were six guys smoking a small joint no bigger than two pieces of pine straw combined. A mosquito leg, they called it.

When I finished showering, I noticed several sets of eyes peering intently in my direction as I walked back to my rack. They were trying to figure me out, checking for any hints or signs of whether I was good people or one of the warden's planted snitches. I sensed there would be trouble heading in my direction before the week was out. I was not going to be relative to their illegal dealings and gambling, so that instantly made me an outsider. And an outsider usually brought down the house with police. It was at this moment that I knew I could not walk around with shower slides on. Even while taking a nap, I kept my shoes tied on tight, always ready for a sneak attack.

All that night, I slept in short intervals, waking every twenty minutes to keep my eyes on the prowling men who just would not fall asleep no matter how late the night wound down to. They reminded me of red-eyed raccoons sneaking into my garbage for treats.

At eight the next morning, I was called to the job board and issued a new job. The farm squads were filled up, so I was given a job in the kitchen, effective immediately. The first day in the kitchen was only an hour-long orientation. Afterwards, I headed to the weight pile to build back up what I had lost in lock-up. On my way past the basketball court, what seemed like a flailing seagull danced in my corner vision. Turning my head to see what had snared it, I saw that it was not a seagull but someone from segregation bouncing a paper pole up and down to attract attention.

The struggle I endured in the Mexican jail brought sympathy for the fisherman. Whereas before, I walked right past it and never gave a single thought to the dangling object. I fast-walked to the cell and picked up a few food items to trade off for a bugler and coffee ball. Returning to the paper pole, I looked around alarmingly for an officer before shoving the cigarettes, coffee, and matches up the paper's orifice. It was a tight fit because I did not take the stamps and note. He could save that bait for another fishing expedition. I jerked on the string to let the fisherman know he had a bite, then proceeded to the weight pile without looking back. It actually felt good to help someone for a change.

I was in a bit of luck because most of the men lifted weights earlier in the day, so there were plenty of weights lying around. I loaded two hundred pounds on the bench press and lifted it off the rack with ease. When the weight touched my chest, a shadow crept over my face. Someone had eased over me with some sort of malign intent.

"Move dat weight and dat's gonna be the last move you make," the stalker threatened.

For a second, I was stunned. Sweat broke out on my forehead, and adrenaline surged through my muscles with an electric fury. I was primed to fight, not cower in the face of a threat. This was real, and the action was about to get kicked up a whole *nother* notch. I pressed the weight up with all the power I could muster and racked it in one blinding motion. The stalker laughed, and I recognized the laugh immediately.

"What's up, dere, teenager?" Willie asked while extending his hand for some Southern dap.

He was truly unaware of the ass-whooping he was about to receive had I swung first and looked later. As the tension eased away from my body, I smiled and gave him one of those ghetto handshakes that always came with a one-arm hug.

"Maaan, what's up, old timer? It's good to see you," I said.

"It's good to see you too, teenager. Man, you been back dere in dat hole so long I thought you had done died off on me."

"N'all, man, but I sure as hell felt like I did dem first couple of weeks on green level. Shiiit, dey had me so starved my stomach started eating my intestines."

Willie laughed open-mouthed, showing a few missing teeth in the back. His face wrinkled enough to reveal his slowly aging marks along his brow. We discussed the goings-on of the past month and a half while working intensely on the weight pile. By the time the sun dipped behind the clouds and the sergeant announced yard closed, I basically knew everything that had occurred while I was in lock-up.

Halfway to the cell, Willie told me to walk slowly so that he could have enough time to run to his dorm and give me a couple of sandwiches.

"Oh no, I'm straight. Hell, I just spent over fifty days in seg, surviving on bread and water."

"That's da problem," Willie said. "You done lost too much weight, and you need to eat all you can to gain your mass back so that you'll be ready to see your folks when you come off restriction. You don't wanna look like no damn POW out dere on da yard. It'll spook yo' mamma half to death. Plus, I don't want ya borrowin' nuthin' from those punks up dere, 'cause dey gone want repayment in all ways you can't imagine."

I stopped arguing because I knew once Willie had his mind set on something, there was no changing it. And then there was the fact that a grilled chicken sandwich was something I had been craving for weeks.

Trotting up the steps to the hot dorm made me realize how much I despised sleeping in it. These were some of the wickedest men society could drum up in one place, and they all had hidden agendas and schemes they hatched daily. The dry blood smell and raucous yelling created a sleepless, watchful environment that was not designed for the fragile. Since it was Friday night, the dorm was confusedly noisy.

Prison-made wine, weed, and large cups of coffee had the men rowdy with a savage thirst for violence and trouble. There were quite a few caffeine freaks who scooped ice into large cups. They would pour an entire 2.2-ounce bag of coffee on top of the ice. A Coca-Cola was poured on top of the coffee and ice to create a potent, all-night elixir that the prisoners called beer. Regardless of the high number of men who were sent to healthcare to have kidney stones removed from drinking excess amounts of caffeine, they still refused to kick or even tone their habits.

After getting out of the shower, I ate a chicken sandwich and tried to get some shuteye. Drunken men beating on boxes and rapping as though they were being paid to perform in a concert would not let sleep happen. Besides the rap groups, there was a dice game going on three aisles down from my bunk. Sleep was not going to be possible at the moment, so I grabbed a half-finished book from under my mat and read. Every time an uproarious noise bellowed out from somewhere in the dorm, I would peek up from the pages to make sure the threat of danger was not approaching in my direction.

A loud "Hell nawl!" was angrily screamed from several voices at the dice game. I quickly averted my gaze in the direction of the commotion.

"Ain't no fuckin' way you finna leave wit all dat money and don't give a nigga no chance to win his money back," a drunken-voiced gladiator yelled from the middle of the throng.

Emerging from out of the huddle was an energetic-looking guy carrying an armload of coffee and cigarettes. He did not have a shirt on, and a scraggy patch of hair covered his flat chest. Turning around to face the losing party, he chuckled wickedly before bragging.

"It ain't my fault y'all niggas ain't got no luck. Shit, if y'all can't respect da loss, den quit gambling."

"So dat's how you gone cut da game up, my nigga? Just take a mufucka money and run, huh?" the guy with the drunken voice asked angrily.

His eyes were angry red, and I could tell his self-contained temper was about to explode like a missile on a target. The hairy-chested guy had little patience. He seemed to be short on explanation and quick on action. But this time, he should have been long on explanation and short on words of action. He cockily answered back with the wrong words.

"Hey, my nigga, if you don't like it, den getcha some straightnin'."

Maybe he was calling a bluff or something, but whatever his intentions, I'm pretty sure he did not expect a reaction. Before the words were fully out of the guy's mouth, the man with the drunken voice and another guy—obviously someone who wanted some of his money back too—approached old Hairy Chest and attacked him with the viciousness of a ravished rattler discovering a nest of baby birds.

The first blow sank into Hairy Chest's jaw with a resounding thud. Coffee and cigarettes clattered to the floor, but surprisingly, no one moved to retrieve them. Hairy Chest stumbled back two steps from the impact of the blow before he recovered. Fuming and juiced with adrenaline, he ran up under Drunk Voice, slamming him to the ground with enough force to snap a backbone. Before Hairy Chest could get in a single blow, the silent partner landed a well-aimed punch into the baggy tissues of Hairy Chest's eye. I looked around frantically for his help, but no rescue came. I suspected this was due to jealous hatred.

Silent Partner reared back for another crushing blow but was stunned by a punch to the gut from a blindly thrown shot by Hairy Chest. Even though Beery Voice was on the bottom, his hands were not pinned down, and he was swinging for all he was worth at Hairy Chest's face. One of those wild blows connected on the nose, and blood streamed from it thickly, dripping back down on his face in sickening spatters. Despite the blood and puffy eye, Hairy Chest was still trying to put up a fight—brutally losing, but fighting on, he continued.

I wanted to stay out of it, but after seeing the murderous bloodlust in the eyes of the crowd watching, I knew no one was going to stop it. Without thinking of the consequences, I jumped off my rack and ran to the slaughter. Seeing that I was about to stop it, a few angered voices yelled out angrily.

"Stay da fuck outta dey business, nigga!"

Ignoring the angry mob, I grabbed Silent Partner and pulled him away from the fight. He was breathing hard and tired, so he didn't put up much resistance. Suddenly, someone at the front of the dorm yelled that heat was coming and to break it up. Two men grabbed Hairy Chest and Beery Voice, then scattered in different directions.

"What da fuck's going on up here?" the officer screamed.

In unison, the men at the front of the dorm yelled out, "Oh, ain't nuttin', officer. We just up here getting crunk on dis rap battle."

"Well, y'all need to keep dat shit down, 'cause I don't feel like hearing shit tonight. If I have to come back in here, I'm lockin' da whole dorm down for a week."

One of the men replied that he was gonna make sure the noise stayed down and that he was gonna keep control of the dorm. Of course, these men were just saying anything to get the officer to head back downstairs. No one wanted to be restricted from moving around the camp because it tied up their money and hustle. Or worse—get hit with a surprise shakedown where weapons, drugs, and julep would be discovered in the dorm.

When the men returned to what they were doing, I noticed the cigarettes and coffee were no longer on the floor. They seemed to have vanished through some magic means by the great David Blaine.

I can't say who scooped the items up, but I'm sure it wasn't Hairy Chest, for both of his eyes were swollen shut. The rest of the weekend melted by without a sign of him. I was beginning to think he had caught protective custody—until Sunday night.

On my way to the bathroom, I saw two men standing beside a rack in the back of the dorm. They were trying to awaken someone who was completely hidden under the covers. Curiosity ate away at me like a migraine aggravation. I eased over to the vicinity with slick caution. Just as the figure emerged from under the covers to see who was handing him something to eat, I managed to catch a brisk look at the hideous creature and stepped back in shock.

A second look afforded me a better view, revealing the ghastly face of old Hairy Chest. His eyes resembled rotted purple grapes, and his nose was crooked and curved like a disastrous highway bend. Blood-soaked tissue was crammed into each nostril, resembling red beams on assault rifles aiming for the jugular. Blistered splices on his lips looked ready to rupture at the first crackle of a smile. A shudder raced through my body as if I, too, could feel the pain.

I wondered to myself why he chose to hide under the covers instead of seeking immediate medical attention. As if on cue, the reason hit me with the hurtling speed of an eighteen-wheeler. Some of Silent Partner and Drunk Voice's homeboys had obviously approached Hairy Chest with a scary ultimatum—either stay in bed while they fed him until his wounds healed or make an attempt to report the incident, in which case further repercussions would be carried out, even if he hid out in segregation.

In his condition, option one was the better choice for him. But damn, it was going to take at least a month for those wounds to heal. By that time, bedsores would have set in. He didn't have long to endure his painful recovery.

Monday morning, when beds had to be put together in inspection order, the dorm officer got a look at his face during one of his usual walkthrough rounds.

"Goddamn, son! What da hell happened to your face?" the officer asked.

Hairy Chest answered back with a textbook lie. "Oh, I fell down the steps."

While the obvious lie was still tumbling from Hairy Chest's swollen lips, the officer was already on his radio calling for the sergeant. I went ahead and grabbed a novel out of my box because whenever a superior was called, a strict lockdown was imminent.

As predicted, Sarg, along with two minions, stepped into the dorm, took one long look at Hairy Chest's face, and issued a lockdown call.

"Now, who did this shit to yo' face, and why has this not been reported?" the sergeant demanded in a super authoritative voice.

Stupidly, Hairy Chest answered back. "I told your officer I fell down da steps tryin' to catch the store draw before dey shut down. That's all to it. Ain't no problem in heah wit me. If it was, I would report it so I could get some help."

Without any patience for being undermined, Sarg angrily ordered for him to be locked up until the truth came out.

"Go ahead and put the cuffs on him, 'cause he's goin' to lock-up for lying to a D.O.C. official."

As Hairy Chest was being led out of the dorm, Sarg reared on her heels to face the dorm and issued her wrath.

"Y'all can sit here and act like ain't nuthin' happened to dis inmate, but I'm getting to the bottom of dis. Everyone is to remain on their racks until I get some names. I don't care if I get 'em by note or if you whisper it to another officer and he tells me. But I want some names."

She then said those magic words that made snitches come out of the woodwork.

"There will be no televisions, microwaves, store draws, or yard calls until I'm satisfied."

Before the day was out, appliances were back in the dorm, and the perpetrators were suffering in segregation. I knew it wouldn't be long before someone snitched because most men couldn't live without the television, microwaves, or yard calls. If asked to read a book, they would flee as if the Devil himself was behind them. Reading within these walls was an original sin to most inmates.

My shift in the kitchen started at twelve p.m., and I was relieved to be away from the dorm. Men from all over the prison worked there, so it was inevitable for animosity to arise. The dishwashers were jealous because the cooks stole all the edible food, and the table wipers were angry because they worked the hardest. It seemed like someone got fired almost daily and was reassigned to the farm because of an envious individual who wanted to fill their slot.

Despite all the hating and snitching, the slickest crooks still managed to empty out the kitchen. They stole yeast to make julep wine. Chicken, fish, tuna, and hot dogs sold for an item apiece, and bleach balls for clothes washing went for two items. There was nothing that couldn't be stolen. Even when the freezers were locked, men would wait for the steward to unlock the door to retrieve something. The moment he turned his back, whole loaves of light bread were lifted and taken down the hallways to make sandwiches to sell.

There were special shakedowns every time a worker left the kitchen, but the officer performing the search would have his palms greased with a couple of packs of cigarettes. This way, pounds of peanut butter, sugar, yeast, and chicken sandwiches were easily boosted from the kitchen. These men had no remorse for whether the rest of the inmates ate or not. When the hard-worked farmers arrived back at camp to eat, roguish men were the reason they were deprived of a full meal.

To make matters worse, my yard time was severely shortened. Men were stealing so much that kitchen cleanup duties were neglected until the last minute, resulting in hourly overlays on a weekly basis.

Apart from harsh weather, the kitchen was turning out worse than the farm. Early the next morning, I caught up with my G.E.D. instructor and practically begged for my old job back. He told me some tutors were on the transfer list and that I would be notified as soon as one left. It could have been paranoia, but I sensed a lying hesitation in his voice. I knew then that talking in prison got a man nowhere. Palms had to be greased, and egos had to be catered to.

The kitchen was only the beginning of a very stressful week. Following the investigation of the fight, the dorm became hotter than a pizza oven. During the day, men were randomly chosen for surprise shakedowns, putting everyone with contraband in a jittery panic. The hottest men—those who smoked and violated daily—scrambled frantically to dispose of their prohibited goods. Even when close to being caught, they refused to trash or flush their goods. Instead, they risked getting another man hit by stashing their contraband in and around other inmates' belongings without their knowing. It was cruel, but it was prison.

I made it a habit to check under my mattress every day and to look in every hole in my mattress to make sure it was clean of someone else's contraband. I didn't want to be sleeping on a bomb and not know it. A "bomb" was the term used when an illegal stash was placed in a neighbor's property without his knowledge.

Every night around midnight, five to ten men would be shaken out of their sleep to take urine tests. It was done this way so no one would have time to prepare ways to beat the test. Once again, bribe payments were made, and most men were notified within hours of a urine test, easily passing it by one of the conventional means of craftiness.

There were plenty of ways to deceive a test, but the two most commonly used were these: take water pills and drink a few gallons of water to flush out the system. The second method, which was purely repulsive, was to dip two fingers in powdered bleach, then urinate off the fingers. Supposedly, the bleach would destroy whatever pollutants showed up. I don't know how truthful it was, but men I saw smoke several times daily always passed the urinalysis with flying colors, and they swore by these two methods as the most likely way to pass a urine test.

On Thursday night, I was shaken awake by a sudden violent jolt. With fists clenched, I sat up with a drunken weariness, staring into the cold and steady eyes of the third-shift officer.

"Grab your I.D. card and head to the shift office. They waitin' on you now to take your piss test."

He stood there for a second longer to make sure I was awake before heading to the next rack. I rinsed my mouth out, then fast-walked to the shift office, hurrying to get there before the rest of the men. Entering the hallway, I saw that it was too late. Men were running from other cells to get spots at the front of the line. By the time I arrived, the line was fifteen men deep, so I knew I was going to be pulling an all-nighter.

By twelve forty-five, only five men had gone inside to urinate. Every man who went inside seemed to be in there for hours. Each time the next man went in, the rest of the line would tell him to hurry the fuck up—just piss in the cup and come out.

The men who had taken water pills and drank a couple of gallons of water performed fidgety little dances to keep their fully extended bladders from exploding where they stood. Finally, around one thirty a.m., I was called inside to urinate. After handing the officer my I.D., I took a studious look at him and discovered what was taking the men so long to finish. He had on a pair of glasses thick enough to restore a blind man's vision. It must have taken him five minutes to write down my information—first holding my I.D. to his nose, then extending his arm out to read it.

"Okay, Rivers," he grumbled. "I want you to step in dat dere bathroom and fill dis here cup at least halfway. When you finish, don't flush da toilet and don't touch anything in da bathroom. Is dat understood?"

I answered yeah, then grabbed a plastic cup. When I stepped into the bathroom, he followed behind me.

"I may be sleepy, officer, but I don't need your hand to help me piss in a cup," I told him.

"Well, I'm just gone stand heah to make sure you don't try to rig up nuttin' in dat cup."

Hateful words sat on the tip of my tongue, but I wasn't trying to take another trip to that Mexican jail from hell. When I got back to the dorm, it was after two. My eyes were so heavy with sleep they had narrowed to feral slits. Pulling my covers back, I realized my wave cap was missing. Drowsily, I shambled to the bathroom to check the mirror while I tied my hair down to keep my waves intact.

The second I stepped inside, something moved in the corner of my eye. A mass of flesh, shifting in a rhythmic motion. My first thought? Someone was waiting for me, probably thinking I was the one who snitched to get the appliances back. I turned my head so fast I nearly gave myself whiplash, teeth clenched, bracing for a blow.

What I saw was worse than a sucker punch.

Four men were crammed into a corner, tangled up in a lurid mess. One was masturbating while two others were locked in a threesome. The hot-railer—the guy who was supposed to be keeping watch—was too busy getting oral sex to do his job. None of them even acknowledged me. They didn't have to. I was out of there faster than a bullet from a fully automatic machine gun.

On my way back to my bunk, I passed the officer heading toward the bathroom.

"God damn!" he yelled. "Y'all cut that shit out! Y'all back here killin' that boy!"

The foursome, knowing they were about to go back to lock-up, must have kept going because the officer shouted again. Then, unexpectedly, one of them spoke up, his voice shaky.

"Jus-Just one mo' minute, officer. We'll be through in one mo' minute."

I laughed so hard my insides ached. A few inmates sat up in their bunks, confused about what was going on. Through a blurred stream of tears, I caught sight of the officer pulling out his nightstick.

"Damn it, I said pull out!" he yelled, furious.

He gave them a few seconds before charging into the bathroom. Two men bolted out, and a third screamed in agony. I suspected the officer had cracked him in the leg because when he finally limped out, he was dragging one foot behind him. By now, half the dorm was awake, watching the mess unfold. Three other officers rushed in, but the chaos was already over. Everyone involved in the "sexcapade" was taken to segregation without hesitation.

Strangely, three of them were back within five days. The one who got hit? He got slapped with trumped-up charges—assault on an officer and some other bogus write-up to keep him in lock-up. The sad truth? If they had been caught smuggling peanut butter or hotdogs from the chow hall instead, they'd still be sitting in lock-up, looking at a minimum of forty-five days. But for whatever reason, the system barely punished men caught in homosexual mischief. Somewhere in the rules, the system secretly condoned it.

After two weeks in that hot dorm, I thought I had seen it all. But what happened next was beyond disgusting.

Some clown, either pissed off or playing a twisted prank, went into the bathroom and took a shit in one of the sinks. To this day, my blood boils just thinking about it. No matter how much they cleaned that sink, I never used it again.

That Friday night, I went to brush my teeth. Just as I squeezed out the toothpaste, I noticed fudge-brown smudges on the sink closest to the wall. The rancid smell confirmed my suspicions, but I had to see the evidence.

When I did, my anger flared like a hissing cat. That was it for me.

The following Monday, I wrote a request to the warden and the captain, demanding to be removed from the cell block. I cited the inhumane conditions as deplorable and unjust. I even stated that if I wasn't moved, I was on the verge of resorting to violent acts. The request was denied as quickly as it was sent out.

My rage hit an all-time high. Something had to give. The only relief I could think of was the chapel. Even that felt like a long shot because prison chapel attendants had a reputation. Being known for attending church was enough to land you on the wrong end of a sharpened blade.

Most people might think it's harsh to slander churchgoers, but they'd change their minds fast if they knew what really went down in the prison chapel. First, they'd have to understand how prison social classes worked. The system was the same everywhere. The more serious your charge, the more respect you had. The lowest of the low were treated like bottom-feeding scum—child molesters, rapists, and other sex offenders.

It did a sex offender no good to lie about his charge. Bed rosters were stolen from the officers all the time. Beside every sex offender's name, there was an "S."

Survival in prison was ten times harder for them. Most men in prison had wives, children, or girlfriends. That's why they despised anyone who had committed a cowardly sexual crime.

Sex offenders were preyed on like South African poachers. They were raped, beaten, and robbed without remorse. To survive, they banded together, seeking protection from the chaplain and warden. As long as they stayed deeply involved in the church and attended a certain number of meetings each month, they were assigned to a dorm designed specifically for their safety. It was called the faith-based dorm, mostly housing pedophiles and men too scared to stand alone. Even the warden treated them differently, giving them special visits, extra incentive packages, the final say on Friday's movie selection, and unlimited access to the television area.

These men were labeled model inmates—examples of positive reformation. But those of us living in the prison knew the truth. More perverted acts happened in that dorm than in the rest of the prison combined. Even female officers hated working there, complaining about the excessive masturbation.

I knew that attending chapel would make men distance themselves from me, but I didn't care. I only talked to five or six guys anyway. I needed help, and help was what I was going to seek. Still, that nameless voice in the back of my head kept whispering, *Why do you want to attend a church run by the sanctimonious?*

All I could remember was a scripture I had read long ago: *Who am I to judge men for their faults?* The Bible was right, so I took heed.

Sunday morning, I made sure to be one of the first inside the chapel. There was an order to the place—nothing like the savage conditions in the rest of the prison. It was fairly new, too. Huge. About forty freshly varnished benches were arranged strategically for maximum seating. The pulpit was large enough for the choir, a full band, the preacher, and his guests, all without anyone feeling the next person's body heat. Just standing there, taking it in, was solace enough.

Church started with a beautiful harmony from the choir—ex-songbirds from the free world. A visiting minister delivered a sermon about enduring hardship and remaining a good father despite being in a place where even family often turned their backs on you. The whole message was moving. I actually found myself feeling uplifted.

Then, thirty minutes before service ended, things took a turn.

Guests on the front row started blowing into huge horns. The drummer pounded obsessively on his set. Half the choir jumped up, running and hollering all around the church. I was the only one not shouting, and it made me feel out of place, like an uninvited family member showing up to the reunion. It took everything in me not to bolt out of there.

After service, a few men from around the camp approached me, flashing fake smiles and welcoming me to the chapel. Just by watching how they carried themselves, I could tell who was serious about their faith and who was just playing along—jailhouse religion.

Plenty of inmates committed to Jesus behind bars but went right back to their old ways once they hit the streets.

Not even an hour after church let out, some of the same men who had just greeted me were back walking with their boyfriends, hustling, and indulging in the kicking-it game. Had it not been for that scripture about not judging, I would have called them out without hesitation.

That night, after the eight o'clock count, ten men who held Bible study and prayer call invited me to their meeting. I went the first night but told them I couldn't make it on Monday. Instead of accepting a polite "no," they pressed me for a reason, quoting scripture and saying things like, "*You should always have time for the Lord,*" and "*When the Lord returns, He won't put your fate on hold.*"

I felt my anger rise, the skin tightening over the bridge of my nose in a menacing frown. I must have looked like steam was about to shoot from my ears because I snapped.

"Look, man, y'all coming over here all aggressive and shit, trying to force a man to go to church. A man goes to church when *he's* ready, not when *you're* ready. Y'all say y'all men of God? Then y'all should *know* that."

My temper, mixed with the weight of pressure, was getting the best of me. I should have left it at that. But I couldn't help myself. I had to get in one last cheap shot.

"Most of y'all going to that church ain't nothing but child molesters and conniving swindlers anyway."

The moment the words left my mouth, I regretted them. I wanted to cup my hands over my lips and snatch them back.

The guy holding the Bible stood there, stunned, his jaw slack, words frozen in his mouth.

"Now that's cold, brother. Real cold words to say to people trying to help you get your faith in the right place."

They turned and walked away. I felt pretty damn guilty, especially since they left without even trying to argue.

Later, after Bible study ended, the same guy I had lashed out at earlier approached my rack. Before he could say anything, I apologized. He told me it was okay—that he understood the place of pain I was coming from. He said they had prayed for me after my outburst and that the good Lord was working on molding me into a man of God. Smiling cheerfully, he looked me in the eyes and told me I was always welcome to join them whenever I needed some encouraging, uplifting words to move my spirit.

A week later, I started going back to the chapel, sinking deeper into the Word each day. Once the church regulars saw how seriously I studied the Bible, they began associating with me on a deeper level. Every one of them claimed to be a prophet, faith healer, or pastor.

The false prophets roamed the camp, supposedly foretelling men's futures and warning them of bad things to come unless they changed their lives. The faith healers were even worse—praying over the sick and promising their illnesses would be gone by morning. But the *tongue talkers* were the worst of all.

Every day, like clockwork, they gathered in the middle of the yard at lunchtime. Some held hands while others were hunched over on all fours. For an hour straight, they mumbled an undecipherable mess of erratic gibberish. It was all just a big show—pretending to be holy.

A few times, they asked me to join them. Every time, I shut them down with a quick *no*. I would rather have no religion at all than gamble with my soul by faking it for the Lord.

The more I attended chapel, the less I wanted to be there. Everywhere I looked, the regulars were scheming—using the Lord's name to hustle food and stationery items. But despite the crooked heathens, I kept going. I told myself I was there for *my* salvation, to serve the Lord—not to get distracted by the hypocrisy around me.

But sex was the final straw.

One Tuesday morning before lunch, I went to the chapel, looking for some peace and cool air. Before I could take two steps inside, I saw two men having sex on one of the back benches. They scrambled into seating positions, trying to play it off like they were just talking, but they were too slow.

I shook my head in disgust, letting them know they were a disgrace to the church before walking out—for the last time.

I was better off studying the Bible with someone *serious* inside the cell block.

Now I understand why inmates get treated with cold bitterness when they start talking about Jesus.

Chapter Twelve

The men were becoming increasingly violent as my final two weeks in the hot dorm began to wind down. There seemed to be no limit to their wrath. Even the officers were in danger of being jumped. It was rare for an inmate to attack an officer because heavy charges were piled against them. They were given free-world assault charges, to which a judge gladly tacked on fifteen years to a previous sentence.

The rise of peer pressure and gang violence among the newer hot dorm inmates was the main cause of the extra surge in tension. Some of the higher-ranked gang leaders often sent crash dummies—low-ranked gang members—on suicide missions. If they wanted someone slapped, stabbed, or beaten, the crash dummies were elected. There was no mission too great for them because these men were willing to do anything to prove they had heart. When one of the "by-the-book" correctional officers was chosen as a mission, I was not surprised.

It all started when an officer wrestled an inmate to the ground and discovered a fifty-dollar pack of weed in his possession. The following day, when the officer returned to work, he was given pure hell the moment he entered the cell. Within an hour, he was pissed, frustrated, and totally out of character.

A crash dummy, who was intensely monitoring the situation, took advantage of the officer's frenzied temper. He intensified the officer's rage with words that were sure to make any man snap.

"Hey officer, while you draggin' yo miserable ass up in here every day workin' all dis overtime, you need to be sneakin' in on yo wife. See who she slidin' dat pussy to since you ain't never dere."

Those words hit like a spitting cobra, ejecting its venom without striking. A rabid bout of fury ignited in the officer's eyes. His mouth twisted downward, and his clenched fists opened to show the fleshy undertones of his palms. Moving at the speed of an eye blink, the officer slapped the crash dummy hard enough to send spit flying halfway across the dorm.

The crash dummy recovered quickly and continued to play off the officer's emotions.

"Okay, I see you wanna try some punk-ass shit, slappin' a nigga behind da protection of dat aluminum-ass badge."

Stepping beyond the call of duty, the officer became ensnared in the crash dummy's play.

"So dis what you want, lil punk-ass mufucka? I'm gon' do better than take off my badge—I'm gon' take da radio off too, and you still won't do shit."

Angry white pockets of foam appeared in the corners of the officer's mouth as he placed his badge in one pocket and the radio in the other. Standing face to face, the crash dummy tightened his belt, then said, "Oh, I'm about to beat yo ass today. Show you dat you ain't gon' be puttin' yo hands on just anybody's child."

"Quit stallin'," the officer said. "I done already slapped da taste outta yo mouth. Now let's see what you gonna do, bitch-ass nigga."

By now, the entire dorm was crowded around them because it was an inmate's dream to witness an officer getting his ass kicked.

"Whoop dat house nigga's ass!" the inmates yelled over the tier to the crash dummy.

I must give it to the officer. To stand there, still willing to fight after being surrounded by an entire dorm of hostiles, was old-fashioned prison rules—a tradition long broken by the new-age wussy cops and rule changes that mandated sentences in excess of fifteen years for hitting an officer. This officer standing his ground was either fearless or too crazy with rage to even realize the threat he was facing.

Suddenly, the crash dummy took a step back and swung with enough momentum to crack a rhino's skull. Unfortunately, his slim stature and lack of strength reduced the potency of the blow. It landed with a solid smack above the officer's right eye, splitting the flesh fold on contact.

The officer staggered into a bunk, then rebounded with surprising speed. Crash Dummy landed two more swift blows on the forehead of the rushing bull, showing a magnificent display of fisticuffs. Once again, his weight failed him. The officer kept charging, possessed as if no blows had ever been thrown. He ran into Crash Dummy like an all-pro NFL linebacker, slamming him between the top and bottom of an iron rack. They both stumbled over the bottom bunk, but the heavier officer landed on top.

Stunned a bit from the fall, the officer began swinging wildly at Crash Dummy's face. Crash Dummy tried to fold his arms across his face for coverage, but the powerful blows were breaking through his noodle arms with ease.

The inmates were not going to stand by and let the officer continue bashing in their homie. Two men grabbed the officer by the shoulders, dragging him backward off Crash Dummy. A few hard-bottomed state boots flung out, thudding into the officer's ribcage.

"Let me go! Let me go! I said getcha gotdamn hands offa me, muthafuckas!" the officer screamed, his voice laced with fear and rage.

The authority in the officer's voice caused them to let him loose, and they all fell back into the crowd of onlookers to avoid catching a new case for assault. The officer stood up, his open wound dripping like a blood-soaked towel. He turned toward the front gate and speed-walked to the entrance, his head flicking from left to right, alert for any sneak attacks. He fumbled nervously with the ring of keys before inserting the right one into the lock, then slammed the heavy iron door so hard it rattled with the spooky clang of crushed metal during an earthquake.

Not quite a full minute later, the rhythmic drum of a soldier's march echoed through the halls. A key clinked in the lock just as a coarse voice yelled in the distance, "Open that muthafuckin' door now!"

From way in the back of the dorm, someone yelled a warning for everyone to catch their racks because the Goon Squad was storming in. Several men in the midst of the melee hollered back that they weren't going anywhere—it was about to go down. More voices piped up, telling the officers to tone it down when they came in because they weren't about to let their frat brother get jumped on after the officer called out the one-on-one and swung the first blow.

From the looks of things, I was about to get caught in a real riot. I had heard numerous stories from older inmates about prison riots lasting for days. I sure as hell didn't want to experience one for myself. The tales of horrid deaths, gruesome maimings, and disgusting acts of rape were crazy enough to keep me in compliance. I jumped on my rack and sat up to catch a bird's-eye view of the action.

The door swung open, and the first face I saw was the bloodied officer. He was now wearing a white T-shirt with polka-dot blood specks all over the front. Behind him, the sergeant and about fifteen other officers marched in, their contorted expressions resembling maniacal terrorists. They gripped their billy clubs and cans of mace, a clear show of riot control and intimidation.

"Just point the son of a bitch out!" the sergeant yelled.

Crash Dummy was still standing between the two racks where he and the officer had fought, his eyes locked in a panic-stricken gaze of terror at the gang in blue. The officer pointed a bloodstained finger at Crash Dummy, and four minions bee-lined toward him with clubs raised. They had murderous intentions of beating him into a bloody mess, but the inmates weren't going to stand for it. Over half the men in the dorm began screaming and charging toward the officers.

"Oh, it ain't 'bout to go down like dat up in here, Sarg! Yo officer swung first, all da inmate did was defend hisself. So if y'all think y'all finna cludge him out, then we 'bout to ride up in here!"

Upon hearing the revolt, the officers turned to face the riotous crowd and resorted to an old scare tactic—hollering at the top of their lungs in unison to strike fear into the inmates.

"GET BACK! EVERYBODY GET DA FUCK BACK AND CATCH YA RACKS NOW! Whoever ain't in compliance gon' get dey head cracked open!"

Instead of running to their racks, more inmates began huddling around the uproarious throng. The sergeant, who just a minute ago had been dead set on putting the works on Crash Dummy, now saw how out of control the situation had become. His bulging eyes and slumped shoulders were clear evidence of overpowering fright.

"Calm down!" he screamed. "Everyone just calm down! Now, ain't nobody gon' be beatin' on nobody! We just gon' handcuff him and take him down to lock-up until the investigation is complete."

An angry stream of air whooshed from the mouths of the club-wielding minions. They were pissed about not being permitted to use the brute force they had been trained to use.

Crash Dummy was roughly handcuffed and practically dragged down to lock-up. It was later learned from the Muslim brothers that he had sustained massive injuries in the confines of segregation. He was taken to a free-world hospital, where he was treated for cracked ribs, broken arms, and a severely gashed head wound. This process was no shock to me—men were beaten on the regular in lock-up. These discreet beatings were a way to eliminate any potential witnesses during the investigation stages.

Despite the heat the men had brought on themselves, the violence continued to escalate. With only three more nights left in the hot dorm, I awoke to what sounded like a herding stampede trampling through the dorm. No sooner had I sat up than a lanky figure zoomed past my bunk, his shower slides smacking against the hard floor—ten times louder than the snoring that echoed clear across the dorm.

Not quite ten feet behind him, a wild-eyed, diminutive figure shot by just as swiftly. A razor-sharp piece of metal glimmered like princess-cut diamonds in the dim light. As the shorter guy wielding the knife closed the gap, the lanky guy began hollering for the officer to open the door. When he got close, he saw that it wasn't open. Instead of beating on it, he ran to the opposite side of the dorm, still screaming for help.

He must have sensed Shorty closing in because he kicked off his shower slides, gaining speed he didn't know he possessed. Lanky might have had a chance at escaping unscathed had he not tried to run a few circles around the middle bunks. While doing so, every light in the dorm lit up, brighter than perimeter searchlights.

Realizing help was on the way, Lanky stumbled clumsily over his own feet, trying to turn toward the door. And that's when Shorty attacked.

"Don't do dis!" Lanky screamed, reaching out to ward off the sword-like blade.

His reflexes were too slow. The blade slashed into the side of his face, plowing flesh from lip to ear. Shorty's second swing tore open Lanky's shirt, ripping a wicked gash across his chest. Lanky squealed like an emaciated calf dying from dehydration and starvation. Desperate to save his life, he lunged and dove into Shorty's midsection.

By the time Shorty's back collided with the floor, four officers were storming through the door. They threatened to use the breath-stealing mace, and Shorty immediately dropped the mini sword. He was wrestled down and handcuffed so tightly I thought his arms would pop from the joints.

Lanky stood back from the ruckus, cupping a flap of skin that resembled a market-cut fillet. The deep slice on his lip percolated with fresh scarlet blood.

"Somebody please help me," he cried sorrowfully. "Dis pie-ass nigga done fucked my shit up!"

An officer grabbed him by the elbow and escorted him to the shift office, grimacing at the wound the entire time.

Shortly after the officers left, I overheard Lanky's neighbor talking about the incident. The whole near-fatal stabbing started over a single pack of cigarettes Lanky refused to repay Shorty. It was crazy, but it happened all the time. Sometimes over things as small as honey buns and coffee.

Three days later, an officer came in with a new bed roster assignment. Relief sawed through my bones when he tapped my rack and told me to pack up.

I was moved to a one-cell unit, which, like the other dorms, operated in its own little enclave. The Blacks dominated, but a few bands of Latinos and Asians were packed in there as well. They stuck together stronger than any other group in the prison. Even the suspicion in their eyes warned that no one outside their circle could be trusted. But it was cool—nobody bothered them, and they didn't mess with anyone either.

Every now and then, some knucklehead looking for trouble would pick a fight with them, hugely underestimating their strength in numbers. Though short in stature, the Latinos and Asians fought like wounded mountain lions turning on their hunters.

One thing I found odd was how many men in the cell block had at least one gold tooth. Even the Mexicans rocked flashy gold. In fact, the amigos had more gold and silver caps than any other race. Through some inquiring, I found out why.

They had a Cuban homeboy among them who specialized in making gold and silver caps. For three packs of Newports, a man could get a custom gold piece made just for his whites. Watching him work was like seeing a master alchemist in action. He took wedding bands, necklaces, and charms, then melted and pounded the gold down until it was thin and malleable. Using an odd mix of tools—fingernail clippers, sandpaper, super glue, and some metallic pieces—he shaped the gold to fit perfectly over a tooth.

Others tried to imitate his craft, but no one could perfect the art like Cubano. The gold-teeth business was a literal goldmine in prison.

The Latinos weren't the only group that dominated one section of the cell. The guys who fell madly in love with each other had their own space, too. They called it their haven for the wedded.

There was no limit to the affection on display in this dorm. Couples showered together, shared meals, and spent the day cuddling, kissing, and fondling one another.

By now, you might be wondering why I use words like "wedded" and "couples" when I talk about these relationships. That's because they took it seriously. They went through all the necessary steps to show their love. They tattooed each other's names on their necks and even held prison marriages.

First, they paid an officer to bring them wedding bands. Once the rings were in, they handmade about twenty invitations for their closest friends. Then they gathered in the back of the dorm, where they exchanged vows. After pronouncing their commitment, they sealed it with a kiss and jumped over a broom to make it official.

One cell was a pornographic freak show for those indulging in prison sex. It was an anything-goes dorm—entirely too much for me. The pimping industry thrived here. More men snuck into this dorm with armloads of items for sexual favors than anywhere else in the prison combined.

That first Friday morning, I met with the bed roster officer in the hallway and talked my way into a new cell. At the 10:30 p.m. bed roster movement, I was relocated to Three Cell. This dorm was structured for model inmates. It was rumored to be the second-most laid-back cell block in the camp, mainly because the older men were true convicts—guys who had been bidding time for 12 to 35 years on a single sentence. They still remembered when prison was about respect and doing your own time. The younger crowd had lost their way. Everywhere else in the prison, everything vile, wicked, and violent was fair game.

Three Cell was the Swedish chalet of Draper. Even the officers who acted rashly in other dorms treated the convicts here with respect. Instead of hollering and cursing through their shifts, they laughed and conversed with the old-timers. Technically, officers weren't allowed to develop friendly relationships with inmates, but the atmosphere in Three Cell defied the rules. They talked about their personal lives with some of the men, played board games, and even brought home-cooked meals for the ones they were closest to.

Unlike the other cells, where TV time was limited to seven hours a day—from 3:30 p.m. to 10:30 p.m.—inmates in Three Cell watched television from the moment they woke up until late into the night. Even the meals were better. The men ate first or second every day, always having hot meals, never having to worry about the edible meats—chicken, fish, tuna—running out before their dorm was fed.

There were so many special privileges that most of the men had grown content with their situations. They laid back every day as if Three Cell was the coziest little getaway in the world. I couldn't blame them. The atmosphere made it easy for anyone without strong ties to the outside world to get lost in the system.

I took advantage of the quiet nights, using the time wisely to think about my kids and my future. Slowly, I began to piece together a plan to accumulate wealth and success. I just needed to figure out which program would give me the parole cut to get home as soon as possible.

Most of the men had been in the system so long they knew every in and out. I started talking to them, trying to find out who I needed to contact to get into a program on the rush. In the process, I learned why some of them didn't even bother trying to go home.

That's when I became aware of the secret business between officers and inmates. In prison, this underground trade was called totting or mule running. For excessive fees, officers smuggled in muscle supplements, steroids, liquor, sweet cigars, drugs—anything small enough to conceal. The inmates had no problem paying the inflated prices because the profit margins were insane.

Drugs were the most lucrative. The money made inside far surpassed street-level hustling. For example, an ounce of low-grade weed sold for $50 to $60 on the streets. In prison, that same ounce cleared $700 easy.

Of that, $300 went to the officer bringing it in, and $400 to the inmate dealing it. And that was just low-grade weed. High-end weed, pills, and harder drugs tripled those numbers.

This explained why men who had used drugs on the streets spent their entire prison bids in a drug-induced oblivion. Getting high became their main focus, not getting out.

The money was too good to walk away from. Some hustlers inside continued taking care of their families—buying furniture, paying bills, even purchasing cars. They were making more money behind bars than most people did in the free world.

Going home wasn't a priority. Everything they wanted was at their whim. Not even sex was hard to get. They threw their money around freely, bribing struggling female officers for favors. Somehow, they always knew which officers were barely staying afloat financially. A couple hundred bucks and—voilà—sex was in the city.

Despite the illegal dealings, Three Cell remained the most laid-back dorm.

Nights were so silent you could hear the faint slurping of a rat licking lard.

I spent those quiet hours filtering through financial success books and the Webster dictionary, soaking my brain with knowledge. I took hundreds of notes, even carried around my own self-created dictionary to memorize words and expand my vocabulary.

It's often said that we are a reflection of the words that flow from our mouths, that speech reveals education and maturity.

My property box, once stuffed with worthless junk, now held notebooks filled with vocabulary words, success strategies, and psychology study notes.

I developed an intense obsession with learning everything about stocks, bonds, IRAs, and mutual funds. I didn't want to leave any business field unresearched. If it involved making money and smart investments that generated residual income and liquid assets, I had to know about it.

As the weeks melted together, I felt like a mad scientist locked away with his own demented experiments. The financial freedom ideas I had conjured up gnawed at me because I couldn't get out to implement them. Days dragged by, and nights passed in restless frustration.

On Monday morning, I went down to the multipurpose building to speak with the instructor of the Crime Bill substance abuse program. The older inmates highly recommended this program, claiming it almost guaranteed a three- to five-year parole cut if completed.

The instructor was a heavyset woman who looked to be in her early forties. Everything about her screamed '60s retro—reddish-brown church-lady wigs, old-fashioned floral print dresses, ebony-black stockings, and jogging sneakers. I had to suppress a laugh to avoid coming off as a class clown. A folded brown bag sat on her desk, and I guessed it contained tuna because her office reeked of it.

A bulky inmate sat in the left corner like a protective gargoyle, ensuring no deranged inmates acted out their fantasies on the instructor.

"How may I help you?" she asked, cutting me off before I could take two full steps into her office.

"I'd like to be placed on the list for your next Crime Bill class."

She leaned back in her chair and asked if I was court-ordered for the program.

"No, ma'am," I told her, "but I'm willing to sign a statement saying I have a drug problem I can't control."

Inmates had to either have a drug-related case or official documentation admitting to substance abuse to qualify for the program.

"I'd like to help you," she said, "but the waiting list is several months long."

Something told me to keep pushing, so I pressed on. I told her about my educational background, my kids, and my loving family who depended on me for support. When I finished, she shook her head, her bottom lip folded inward as if she were deep in thought.

Finally, her eyebrows arched as an idea came to her.

"You say you went to college, huh?"

"Yes, ma'am," I answered without hesitation.

"Are you good at math and reading?"

"Never been a problem for me. Reading's actually my favorite subject, and I was tutoring GED math a few months ago right here in prison."

"Well, that's good," she said. "Because I can bring you in as a tutor while enrolling you in the program at the same time."

"That's fine with me. I need a constructive job anyway, Mrs. Adams."

She told me there were only thirty-four days left in the current class. As soon as it ended, she'd put me on the job board for the next session.

After thanking her, I went back to my cell and started planning my future business ventures.

Chapter Thirteen

The thirty-four days wound down at an agonizingly slow pace. With just three days left on the long wait list, I was placed on the job board list to be placed in the Crime Bill Program. This happened on Friday morning, and by Friday night, I was packed up and moving to the rehab dorm.

The rehab cell was a foreign housing structure dropped off in the middle of purgatory. Instead of cracked concrete floors, a shiny red floor was in its place. The entire dorm was painted a sky blue to symbolize peace and unity among the addicts. On the left was a huge mural of a sun setting above a colorful rainbow, illuminating a large portion of the wall. The twelve steps to recovery and several famous quotes were painted on each pillar, with the words "encouragement" hand-scripted in cursive.

Beside every rack was a workstation complete with desks, drawers, and chairs. With everyone assigned to their own workstation, I knew that my study habits would become extremely diligent. I wasted no time getting my bunk and property in order because I wanted to get a feel for the dorm. After taking a brisk walk through the cell block, I pulled out some research notes and sat down at my desk to go over them. I found it easier to retain the information because the distractions were far fewer than the rugged atmosphere of the regular prison dorms. Despite there being a little over a hundred men in the dorm, the noise level was shockingly minimal. There was none of the wrestling, slap boxing, and kicking games that occurred in most cell blocks because horseplay resulted in termination from the program. The one benefit I enjoyed the most was the absence of late-night bathroom activities. Thank God I didn't have to put up with watching fake daytime gangsters giving the tongue and ass up at night to a member of the sisterhood.

On Monday morning, I found out how these violent men had humbled themselves to these strict rules. As we were preparing for class, Mrs. Adams suddenly appeared in the doorway with a very stern look etched on her face. The wide, felicitous smile that she had so happily sported in orientation would not have been evident had a forensic scientist searched for it.

"Most of you already know me by now. But to the new class who just moved in, I want to go over the rules with you so that when you mess up, there won't be any questions asked when I dismiss you from the program."

All eyes were on Mrs. Adams. I was not surprised at all to see that no one even attempted to "gun her down" (masturbate), because being caught by Mrs. Adams meant severe repercussions. The main one was being denied parole.

There were twenty rules painted above the entrance of the cell, and she explained them thoroughly. Many of the rules were so strict that even I began to wonder if completion of the program was possible. The few that were going to be the hardest to abide by were: no sleeping or sitting on bunks until after four-thirty p.m., no profanity or hollering across the dorm, and no television until the weekends. Just as I was thinking about skimming on the rules, she dealt a deathblow before I could figure out how to outmaneuver her.

"Now, I have elected three dorm aides to keep me informed of the daily goings-on in here, so don't even think about trying to outslick me, because I will find out before God gets the news."

She then turned around to face the gaping crowd. "Absolutely no disciplinaries nor citations while in my program. If you get one, I don't care if it's three days left to graduation or two hours, I'm giving you the boot without hesitation."

I knew then that I was going to have to fly straight for the remainder of the program. About forty-five minutes later, the sergeant made an announcement for the new Crime Bill class to report to the multipurpose building for class.

"You need to get there, get there, gentlemen. Mrs. Adams said one second late and it's over with."

I double-checked my property box to make sure it was locked, then hauled ass to the multipurpose building. As I zoomed out of the cell, I saw a few stragglers who had laid down for a quick nap sit up on their racks. Check-in time was at eight, and I arrived in class with four minutes to spare. Only half the class was there, and Mrs. Adams was not yet present either. As the minutes ticked away, most of the class began dragging in.

At precisely eight o'clock, Mrs. Adams strolled in with an armload of papers and a number of blue folders. Without even looking at the class, she took one look at her watch and muttered aloud to herself.

"Oh! It's eight already. I hope everyone paid attention to the announcement this morning because whoever ain't here might as well pack up their things and move back into population where they came from. I'm not ever gonna start my program off on the wrong foot. People better start realizing if they truly want something, it ain't gonna come easy, and it's my job to make this program a real challenge so you all can grow from it. This is for your benefit, not mine."

Just as she was about to close the door, three late birds tried to enter the class. Mrs. Adams didn't even ask them why they were late. She simply turned them around with a roll of her finger and slammed the door shut with fiery haste. There was a joyful bounce in her step as she walked back to her desk. It was as if she was elated to be depriving men of a chance at early parole for petty reasons. There were other forms of punishment she could have resorted to on the first infraction. She was about as soulless as Adolf Hitler.

"Whew!" she uttered. "The class has slimmed down already."

I'm sure she made a very stern statement in the sand at that moment on where she stood with discipline and her total lack of tolerance for not following directions. Her illustrative action seized everyone's attention, sleepy heads and all.

"I told you all in orientation that I was not to be taken lightly. It's in your best interest to adhere strictly to the rules." She voiced this without a single blink of the eye. A perfect model for a dictator in the Middle East.

Ten minutes later, we were each issued a blue folder containing various papers on the effects of drugs and three books that dealt with alcoholism, drugs, and life stories of recovering addicts. Once everyone was assigned books, Mrs. Adams introduced the class to her aide, then walked out of class. The aide was a previous graduate whose job was to enlighten the class while Mrs. Adams was locked away in her office—taking a break from stressing out on the inmates.

He introduced himself as DeNardo while delivering a swagger of cool confidence. The first rule explained was a quick rundown on Mrs. Adams' "don't-try-me" temper and a warning not to get caught violating any rules in her presence. For the better part of an hour, DeNardo explained the daily routines that were going to start off each day: prayer, fifteen-minute meditation, feeling check, and morning P.T., which was a thirty-minute exercise session to get the blood and adrenaline flowing.

The rest of the day was a breeze. We talked about our lives on the streets and what drug of choice led us to be where we currently were. The white guys' stories were amazing to hear because they tried every means of getting high at early ages just to be rebellious. Some punctured holes in Lysol spray cans and drank the contents when they didn't have enough money for alcohol. Others told stories of being strung out to near death on heroin. Many spoke of staying awake and wired up for upwards of twenty days like spirit-raised corpses on crystal methamphetamine and stealing all of their parents' hard-earned possessions to purchase small amounts of crack.

Now, I must admit that I have been around and dealt with junkies many times before, but rarely had I seen so many youngsters deteriorated and tainted by drugs as I saw that day. They were sixteen, seventeen, and eighteen-year-old youngsters whose futures looked bleak and hopeless because of their refusal to refrain from drugs. If these men were responsible for running our country in the future, then the U.S. better get ready for a flop. There was no ambition even remotely evident in the youngsters' eyes. They carried that chingy, dope-fried look that resulted from withdrawal.

I had to stop myself from pre-judging these men because I fared no better than they did. We were all young and in the same sinking boat of despair, without a paddle, sail, or rescue boat to save us from drowning in the muck of life and our addictions.

The class was so enthralled in telling their stories that we hardly noticed how much time had lapsed until the officers barged in to tally the class for the two o'clock headcount. A hushed silence engulfed the room, as no talking was allowed during count time. No sooner had the officers exited the class than Mrs. Adams entered. Her old flower-print dress swung around her ankles like a tattered sheet curtain blowing with the wind. She announced that class would be over when the headcount was cleared. She also mentioned that because class would be over for the day and she was departing to pick her kids up from school, that didn't mean we were exempt from the rules of the dorm. We would still be governed by the dorm aides and their constantly prying eyes for violators.

In my mind, I was thinking, *this woman is a total control freak*. Or maybe her husband ran the household so tight that she had to exert her anger out on the class to boost her self-esteem. In either case, she was not playing games with this program, and neither was I.

As we began pouring back into the dorm, some men headed straight for their bunks, thinking Mrs. Adams was retired for the day. I remembered the heavy emphasis she had put on the words "just because I'm gone" and opted to sit at my desk instead of lying down. I analyzed everyone I encountered to learn the characters of the people I was living with. I needed to know who wanted to be the teacher's voluntary pet for brownie points. Mrs. Adams struck me as the guile and conniving type and needed too much control to rely on just the dorm aides to do her bidding.

Sure enough, at ten minutes after three, she sneaked up on us. Several men were caught red-handed: sleeping, shirts off and untucked, playing dominoes (which was against the rules only in the rehab dorm). She made it known that she was in the vicinity.

"I see now that this is not going to work. You people evidently think I'm a joke. Right now, I should just kick everybody out and start a new class because I see that you all are a bunch of hardheads."

The officer in charge of the dorm walked in and asked Mrs. Adams what the problem was. She turned on him with a fiery rage and snapped at him for allowing us to break the rules, threatening to brief the warden on the officer's lack of enforcement. She was so caught up in her frenzied outrage that she clearly forgot she was dealing with an officer and not an inmate who was not subject to her threats. The officer put her in her place and told her he wasn't taking any shit from her. A flush of embarrassment fluttered across her cheeks, and her breasts raised in angry heaves as she faced the class with a most hateful gaze before storming out like the Wicked Witch of the West.

The rest of the day, we waited in tense anticipation for the warden to walk into the class and announce for us to pack up. He never showed, but that did not ease my worries. Many of the guys were walking around the dorm saying "fuck Mrs. Adams," and if she wanted to kick them out, then she damn well could because they didn't need the program anyway. These were the short-timers with non-violent cases who were only serving a few months to two years with good time. They were going home regardless of what happened. But the violent crime cases like mine seriously needed this program to make it out before the decade was over.

I glanced over at the three dorm aides who were sitting at the front of the cell, silently soaking up everything said about Mrs. Adams. They were eagerly awaiting tomorrow's check-in call so they could rehash all that was said and by whom to Mrs. Adams.

Class the following morning was a bit drab as we sat in anxious anticipation for Mrs. Adams' arrival to deliver her dismissal speech. I was quite nervous myself about what her decision was going to be with this group. The aide began the day with the routine prayer as if nothing bad was in store for us.

An hour later, class was in full swing and still no sign of Mrs. Adams. We were in a much better mood because the aide informed us that he had spoken with Mrs. Adams in her office and she did not mention anything about rounding up the list of names to start a new class. Most everyone speculated that the reason she refused to show her face was because of sheer embarrassment from what happened with her and the officer. I could have cared less. If it were left up to me, I would have preferred that she be a no-show for the remainder of the program.

My wish was surely denied by the wish maker because Mrs. Adams stumbled into class with an armload of papers just twenty minutes before count time. She spoke to save face, then began issuing out homework assignments to be completed by the beginning of class the following day. She was really trying to make it hard on us now. She gave strict instructions for us to drop the assignment on her desk as we entered the class in the morning. For those among us who thought about not completing it, she told them to drop their books on her desk and not worry about coming back. A few men grumbled in protest, but none were loud enough for Mrs. Adams to distinguish who the culprits were.

Flooded feelings of relief seethed through my body when the count was announced clear, and we were able to go back to the dorm. Though tired and sluggish from the long night, I refused to fall victim to the neatly made bunk that was like a desert mirage at the moment. It looked so tempting and comfortable. My eyelids sagged like ten-pound weights were dragging them closed, but I forced them open with fifteen pounds of pressure. I fought a losing battle with sleep for ten good minutes before my head went crashing down on the desk, only to awaken a fully restored hour later.

My body was programmed to the routine goings of the day, so it automatically stirred me awake ten minutes before chow. The winter days were so short that by the time chow was over, the yard was closed if you were the last or next-to-last dorm to eat. Without a watch, the long nights easily became confusing. Seven o'clock seemed like twelve, and twelve seemed like three a.m. Time was fusing together so slowly that I retired to my bunk to hibernate for the night. Right before I closed my eyes, one of the white guys from class walked by and announced he would do homework for one food item. It had been so long since we were issued homework that I had completely forgotten about it. I sat up with an urgent haste, sleep instantly draining from my tired body with the spike in adrenaline.

We were required to read a story on the founder of Crime Bill and answer a three-page questionnaire as we read. I was so tired I skimmed through the story, stopping only to fill in the answer to a question. Thirty-five minutes later, I was snuggling under the covers.

Mrs. Adams was present at the start of class for the first time since the program began. She stood facing the door, analyzing everyone as they walked in to see who had their homework and who didn't. Once we were all seated, she counted the paper stack on her desk to be sure that no one had slipped by her without dropping in his assignment. When all papers were accounted for, she grabbed the stack and walked next door to her office.

Denardo took over the class and began with the morning prayer and meditation as usual. When we arrived back in class from our exercise session, Mrs. Adams was again present. This was odd of her to appear in class twice in the same morning, so I knew something was up. She ordered everyone to close their books and to slide them to our left.

"This is a pop quiz on the reading assignment from last night, and I expect everyone to do well." She spoke with a slick demeanor and even smirked a little before handing out the quiz. Maybe the smirk was just a distorted illusion in my imagination, but it sure as hell fit her well. It was obvious one of the dorm aides had mentioned to her about men paying to have homework done.

This lady was after us with the hounding speed of a cop car, and it did not seem like she was ever going to let up. I wouldn't have been surprised to find out that she had a private vendetta to only graduate two people per class. Rumors were already circulating that she never graduated a full class, and I believed every bit of it. Some of the men who graduated rehab programs under different instructors bragged about the ceremonies they had after completing the program. They never failed to remind us that Mrs. Adams held the smallest and shortest ceremony because of her low number of graduates. While the other instructors paid for a smorgasbord of food out of their pockets, she only allowed food to be eaten if the visitors brought enough for everybody.

As the weeks melted into each other, so did my tolerance for Mrs. Adams. I learned to stay out of her way and remain low-key while in class. Sometimes a person would get caught sleeping or saying the wrong thing in class, and she would subject them to the most embarrassing type of punishment. Because she was such a 'saint,' she did not allow vulgar language to be spoken in her heavenly presence.

One evening, while Mrs. Adams was away in her office, two guys got into a heated argument over whose city projects were the most violent. Not only was it a stupid argument, but it was also pointless. DeNardo tried to calm them down, but their voices only elevated to higher levels, loud enough to filter through the thin walls and into Mrs. Adams' office. Just as one of the guys stood up and began hollering, "Nigga, yo hood ain't shit," Mrs. Adams opened the door to see what all the noise was about. Her eyes were wide open from the shock of the language being yelled as if it was an admittance into her program.

She did not speak. A single wave of her finger was all it took for the guy to understand that he was to follow her out into the hallway. We remained quiet, trying to eavesdrop on what was being said in the hallway. When the violator stepped back in, he looked as if he had seen a ghost. He walked straight to his table, grabbed his books, and placed them on the shelf.

"What'd she say? What'd she say, man? Is she gonna kick you out or what?" one of his partners asked.

"Naw, man. She told me I gotta write 'I won't say nigga again in Mrs. Adams' class' ten thousand times. It's fucked up though because she wants it on her desk first thing in the morning, and that shit ain't even possible. That bitch knows what she's doing. She's seen my court order, and she knows a nigga needs this program to get out in a couple of months on this five-year bid they gave me. If I don't graduate, I'm gonna have to pull some years in this bitch. I ain't tryna do that shit, my dawg. Then this bitch gone say if I don't finish, not to come back because she's kicking me out. These old battered hoes know they step on a nigga's neck when they get the ups on us. That's why I be slaughterin' them bitches in the streets with no remorse, 'cause of old hateful hoes like her."

"Well, don't worry, my dawg. We gotcha. We gonna pull through with ya. Just send a nigga something when you touchdown."

This was how prison was. Men trying to survive by doing favors for short-timers in hopes of receiving monetary support in return when the short-timers get out. Most of the time, these promises are forgotten, and no rewards are earned on the favor gamble. But sometimes, real true bonds are developed, and the short-timers actually find ways to send money back to their caged soldiers, especially the established dope boys and those with good business investments in the streets.

True enough, the violator had three homies stay up half the night writing with him. They each wrote about twenty-two hundred lines apiece, then retired for the night. All in all, they were still a thousand lines short. I guess they didn't think Mrs. Adams was going to count the lines, but boy, were they wrong. They were dealing with a well-precisioned punisher, and she was never to be underestimated.

She enlisted two aides from the other rehab instructors, and together they counted every line. When we returned to class from lunch, the fuming witch was waiting with the papers in hand. We were still settling down when she started her wrath.

"I don't know who you think you are, young man, but I'm not the one to play games with. I just know you're not that dumb to where you can't count. Your file says you were a drug dealer, so I know you can count. So why am I short a thousand lines?"

The violator answered back that he tried to finish, but his fingers started to ache and cramp, so he quit. There was no shaky nervousness in his voice. He was gruff, as if he really wanted to say to hell with this program and this crazy bitch. The severity with which he needed this program was more than likely the only thing keeping his tongue in check.

Mrs. Adams raised her facial features for just a few seconds as if she too could sense the man's anger, but then she quickly recovered.

Well, I want the other thousand lines on my desk first thing in the morning, along with three thousand extra for not completing the assignment in the time allotted to you."

I could hear the air whoosh from his homie's mouth as they knew it would be another long night of coffee and coke on ice. The violator gave Mrs. Adams a spine-chilling look, his eyes fiery red like a demon's tongue. I could imagine the hurt in his chest from swallowing down his words and pride. He was probably a major player on the streets.

I thought about how humiliating it must have been to be the subject of her vengeance and began wondering how much worse it could get. It didn't take long to find out that Mrs. Adams specialized in punitive punishment. For every slip-up, she had a solution. In the corner of her office, there were several laminated white poster boards with idiotic phrases written and drawn on them in brilliant colors. Holes were punched across the tops of each one so that a string could be tied to it and worn around the neck.

Whenever someone was caught sleeping, complaining, or dumbfounded by certain questions, she would make them wear these signs for the duration of twelve to forty-eight hours. The catchy and embarrassing phrases would read something like: *I'm a baby, so where is my bottle? I'm not an idiot: 2+2=7,* or *I'm dumb because I sleep in class.*

The signs had to be worn everywhere: to lunch, back to the cell block, and even to the weight pile if that's where they spent their yard time. Shower time and lights-out were the only reprieve given to remove the signs. If ordered to wear the sign, it was best to comply. It was automatic dismissal for non-compliance. Plus, the 'house niggas' sneaked around like sniveling snakes, watching and waiting for a man to slip up. They figured by telling, they would earn brownie points and an automatic ride through the program without fault.

Surprisingly, I was able to maneuver around for six weeks without being chastised by her. I stayed as far away from her as possible. It was difficult for her to even recall my name at times. I could have kept going like that for the remainder of the program had I not been subpoenaed back to court.

Partway through the sixth week, I received a letter from Dre's attorney that I would be called back to court on his behalf to testify for him at his trial. The date was set for the following week, which gave me just enough time to make arrangements with Mrs. Adams.

The reason Dre was just being tried for the case was that he opted to take it to trial instead of copping out to the robbery charge. I agreed to a plea bargain because I knew I had a slim to zero chance of winning. My two Class A robberies carried a maximum stiff penalty of ninety-nine years apiece, plus twenty-five years for gun enhancement charges on top of that. The racist county we were being sentenced in was known for handing out that time to blacks like it was unwanted Christmas sweaters from the aunt stuck in the seventies.

As I re-read the letter, I tried to come up with reasons why Dre wanted to risk so much time by taking the case to trial. Spending the court's money on a lengthy trial almost guaranteed the maximum fines and penalties. I figured some greedy, overpriced lawyer was filling his head with senseless ways of beating the case just so he could milk him and the church he joined for as much money as possible. The church he joined was saying he was innocent because he never went in the store, so they raised over ten thousand dollars and paid for his lawyer in cash.

As I sat pondering Dre's motive for calling me to trial, the more puzzled I became as to what kind of justice he believed I could render for him. Then a thought came to me: maybe if I lied for him, his chances would increase at beating the case. There was no sense in all of us rotting and aging in prison while our mothers and loved ones wept late at night for our return. The system had enough brothers incarcerated. Why not keep one free of this modern-day slavery? Even though the district attorney often tore apart fabricated stories like corporate paper shredders, I was willing to risk perjury to keep one brother from this hellish plight.

Before the week was out, I informed Mrs. Adams of the day I was subpoenaed to be in court, and she acted exactly as I expected her to—harsh and indifferent. She reminded me of the three days we were allowed to miss when called back to court, putting heavy emphasis on the words *three days only*. No extra days would be taken into consideration for missing class. Rules were rules, and she said she did not bend them for anyone. A day late, and I was out of the program that I worked so hard to complete as a signature statement for a huge parole cut.

I was picked up on a Friday morning by a sheriff deputy and escorted to the Henry County jail. Nostalgic memories reminded me of the fear I felt when I was first placed in this foreign county jail. Racism was pandemic throughout this place, and the county workers did not cloak their feelings about their stance against blacks and Latinos, especially the Mexican immigrants. The time handed out to us versus the slap on the wrist for the whites was not even close to being in line with the harsh sentencing guidelines mandated throughout the criminal court by the three ruthless judges who were famously rumored to have handed out over a million years in sentences before they retired. I was not looking for this trip to be a hayride through Mayberry for me or my co-defendant. I remembered the stern words of the district attorney, who boldly stated at my sentencing hearing how he felt about me and others like me.

"This here ain't some big-time county where criminals get away with a few years for violent crimes. This here is Henry County, and we aim to give you the max sentence."

He told me I was the luckiest son-of-a-bitch alive to get "only" 54 years for my crime, and that if it were solely up to him, I would have gotten the two ninety-nine year sentences plus the twenty-five years for gun enhancement. This was not a place to play poker with the justice system.

The moment I entered the cell block, all eyes feasted on me with fearful gazes. They acted as if I were a monster. I was given a warning by the deputy and the county booking officer not to stir up violence during my stay, or there would be terrible consequences for me. Their fear was injected into the hearts of the inmates as well. I could tell they were intimidated by me because I was being brought back from a ruthless prison society, while they were confined to a small-town county jail where everyone knew each other. I was much bigger and more muscular than when I was first sentenced in this county. My size and my violent crime struck fear into the hearts of these men.

As I began making up my bunk, someone sitting in the TV area yelled out, "Damn Ray, is that you, nigga?"

I looked behind me and recognized the face of a guy I had gotten cool with on my first bid in the county jail. I hollered back at him,

"What up, Cory? Shit, nigga, I thought you were on the streets by now with that short time you had. Man, why in the hell are you still here?"

He walked up to me smiling and gave me that ghetto handshake known by every black man on the streets.

"I did get out, but I caught another dope charge while I was out on bond. Shit, these peckerwoods ain't playin' no more. They lockin' up every nigga movin' any kinda way wrong. They don't give a damn how petty the case is. They wanna get some time up outta your ass down here. Man, I done fucked up for real this time. Everybody mad at me too. Hell, it ain't just me locked back up. Half the niggas you seen on your last bid done got locked back up and sent up the road to the big house."

I shook my head in despair, inwardly wishing I had been granted that second chance that so many knuckleheads were ruining, making it rough on the next man when it came to judgment in sentencing. Their revolving-door crimes didn't do any justice to the stereotypes of young black men characterized as out-of-control urban terrorists.

When lunch was served, my stomach knocked with hunger pains at the sight of seasoned French fries, handmade juicy hamburgers, soft oatmeal raisin cookies, and tropical punch Kool-Aid. This was the one benefit of being in a small-town jail. All the residents knew each other, so they made sure their incarcerated relatives and neighbors got a full hot meal, despite their crime. Outsiders like me got the benefits of this small-town rearing.

I hadn't eaten real beef and thick-cut fries in so long that I almost forgot they existed. Everything on my plate was devoured with savage greed before anyone else was even halfway through with their meal. These guys had never seen a prison entrée, and they were burnt out on this rotational menu served from week to week. To them, this was stale, same-old-same-old food. But to me, it was a buffet laid out for the Almighty creator. They must have felt sorry for me because they offered me helpings of their food with a free-hearted friendliness. Institutionalization kicked in, and I started thinking about how nothing was free in prison. Everything had to be paid for with sex or money. I looked at the tantalizing food hungrily. These sheep weren't predators preying on lame prey. They were down-home folks, I reminded myself, before accepting the extra helpings. What I couldn't eat, I wrapped in tissue for later. The guys in the cell block were staring at me as if I were an aboriginal spectacle at a fair in the early 1900s.

At a little before two o'clock, the deputy came back to escort me to the courthouse. I was taken to one of those cold rooms that were designed to arouse fear and nervousness when interrogated by authority. The district attorney arrived first. He had the same droopy jowls, dumpy waistline, and imitation suit as before when we first encountered each other some years back. I didn't expect him to be any healthier. He was living the small-town boss-hog Dukes of Hazard life—big Texas-sized steaks, vegetables cut fresh from the garden, smokehouse hog straight out the backyard, and free-range chickens from the front yard.

He drilled me with a barrage of questions, which I answered dishonestly to protect Dre's innocence. After he left, fuming without satisfaction, Dre's lawyer strolled in with a cheesy smile spread across his face. I relayed the same innocent story I told the district attorney, and his eyes grew big as golf balls with eager satisfaction.

"We're going to win this case and set Dre free," he said. I was a little more experienced with this small-town justice system, and I wasn't swayed by the conniving pep talk. It was going to take a miracle. One involving God floating down from the heavens to declare him a free man. Any miracle feat under that was just hope and a prayer.

I did not agree with Dre's decision to take the case to trial because we were caught on the scene with all the evidence. I couldn't fully figure out his defense, besides my testimony, but he still had to deal with Hedrick working with the district attorney against him to keep himself free of prison time. It was a game of convincing the jury who was telling the real story—Dre and I saying he was clueless about the robbery until it happened, or Hedrick testifying about the entire planning stage of the robbery, implicating Dre as guilty as charged.

I didn't want to see him lose this case. I saw firsthand how losing a case in this part of redneck country stripped a man of his entire future with one bang of the gavel and a guilty reading by the jury. The maximum sentence was a sealed judgment that often resulted in a life sentence, no matter how petty the case, for a man of color. In our eyes, we were petty first-time criminals; in their eyes, they saw the preservation of superiority. Dre was facing a hundred years plus, and just the thought of it was enough to send a shiver down my spine.

Monday morning, after breakfast, an announcement was made for two other guys and me to get ready for court. We were shackled down like mass murderers and packed into a deputy car tighter than fat toes in a too-small stiletto pump. All I could think about was the outcome of placing me on the stand. Either my story would be believed, or the district attorney was going to dissect it like a forensic scientist and hit me with a perjury charge. My thought process rushed at a million miles per hour, and I became stumped as to which way to proceed—the truth or the lie?

By the time we arrived at the witness room, I had made up my mind to help keep Dre free. I rehashed the altered story repeatedly in my head to ensure there would be no stammering or stuttering when drilled by the prosecution. The other two guys were on the docket ahead of me, so they were taken to the courtroom hours before me. As the hours dwindled down, my anxiety increased. The room became colder than a morgue, my palms began perspiring, and I could feel my heart pounding so loudly it echoed in my ears.

The door opened, and I jerked backward with so much tension that my knee smacked painfully on the underside of the table.

"It's lunchtime," the detective said.

I could feel my digestive system thaw as the built-up tension permeated through my pores. I was escorted back to the county jail to eat lunch, but my appetite was severely lacking because of my nervousness. I forced down what I could in hard-to-swallow lumps and took a five-minute power nap. A tap on my shoulder let me know it was time to head back to that one-room witness dungeon. Right before I was ushered into the witness room, I got a chance to see Dre for the first time in over two years. There was so much worry and agony etched in his face that he seemed ready to burst into tears at any moment. He looked fragile. His eyes were baggy and bloodshot, and he appeared years older. I felt sorry for him. He had made a hard bed to lay in, and there was no cotton around to comfort him during the nightmare.

I sat alone in the witness room with a slight tremble. The lie that I had rehashed over and over was stuck in my brain like plaque. My nerves eased up on the tension as the weakened lie became a predominating truth. The first hour trickled by with the speed of a bullet train, but the three hours that followed crept by with the sluggish crawl of a three-toed sloth.

By the time the officer entered the room, I was drifting in and out of sleep. The haggard look on his face let me know that they weren't going to call me in for the day. On the ride back to the county jail, I managed to ask the officer a few questions about how Dre's trial was coming along. He wasn't able to tell me any specifics, but he did tell me that Dre's lawyer was making a strong defense case in the trial so far.

With that information, I felt a hell of a lot better. The legal massacre I expected the prosecution to carry out from beginning to end was now being jostled back and forth like two Civil War generals mounting their last stands.

When the shackles were off and the cell door was closed, a tranquil feeling of relief soothed my tensed muscles. I felt like I had been working out. To be back in the cell block, away from the hustle and bustle of lawyers, prosecutors, and judges, felt like a turtle shirking into its shell to avert impending doom.

Before I could settle down, Cory wasted no time bothering me with questions about the trial. I was so tired of being interrogated that I was on the verge of exploding with rage. I had to remind myself that it wasn't Cory's fault I was there. I managed to lower my temper for the nosy fellow.

"If I only knew," I told him. "Hell, I didn't even get a chance to hear any trial testimony. The DA's scared to let me hear anything for fear it would structure my story and damage their case, so they've got me locked up in a witness room."

I told him as little information as possible. There were too many cases involving jailhouse snitches volunteering bogus and trumped-up statements against cases they only overheard discussed between co-defendants to get themselves a reduced sentence.

"That's fucked up," Cory responded as if he could do something to remedy the situation.

"Yeah, it is," I replied. "I'll be glad when this shit is all over with, so I can get the hell out of this crazy town."

Chapter Fourteen

The appetite that lay dormant during the day returned to betray me. The hunger pains boiled around in my stomach with a voracious greed, yearning to be supplied with a meal fit for three. The pains increased at the sound of the food cart rumbling through the hallways. Dinner consisted of two pieces of deliciously golden, juicy, deep-fried chicken, green beans, mac and cheese, and two pieces of bread. The elated feeling that a kid gets when stepping into a candy factory overcame me, and I began rubbing my hands together in anticipation of the meal. Not a moment was wasted staring at the food. I tore into it like a famished pit bull, cleansing the bones of every scrap of meat before diving into the mac and beans. Prison taught me to take advantage of every opportunity given. Within the past couple of days, I made sure to act like a starveling at every meal, mainly to gain sympathy from the burned-out county inmates. The ploy worked because I was given extra servings at every meal. Even the snacks bought on canteen commissary were freely offered to me. I know it sounds like a harsh move, but I firmly believed in the Charles Darwin theory at the time—survival of the fittest.

A few hours later, I was sitting at the table playing a game of spades when the local news came on. I was not quite paying attention until I heard Dre's full name and the amount of time he was facing if found guilty. I looked up just in time to catch a snapshot of Dre's dejected, overburdened features as he was about to be questioned by the district attorney. If I did not feel sorry for him then, I sure as hell felt sorry for him now. He looked as if he were standing over a drain, watching his life being flushed down it.

"Whatcha doin' gambling with ya life like that, Dre? Man, just take da damn deal and get back home in a few years."

I was speaking aloud to no one in particular. Cory offered his opinion that Dre might still beat his case because trials in Henry County are usually over in a day. With Dre's case still going, it was a possibility that the district attorney was having a hard time proving his case. Knowing how heavy the evidence weighed against Dre, I did not believe with a fraction of hope that the case was going to be won—not in this infamous county.

Tuesday morning felt like déjà vu. Each day was a routine of the day before. Instinctively, I awoke before breakfast, brushed my teeth, made up my bunk, and started reading a book while anxiously waiting for the call over the intercom to get ready for court. At a quarter past seven, I was shackled down and on my way to that dreaded witness room. This was the third and final day of the trial, and the courtroom was packed with nosey spectators looking for something to gossip about.

"Damn," I said to myself, "out of all the days, the courtroom had to be packed on the day I was to take the stand."

All those eyes alertly watching me—some filled with decades-old racist hatred, and very few present to show support.

Ten minutes before the start of the trial, Dre's attorney entered the witness room and gave me the rundown on the day's proceedings. Since Dre had already taken the stand, he let me know that I was more than likely going to be called to the stand sometime early that morning. My attorney predicted Hedrick would get on the stand immediately after I testified, to take credibility away from my story. Hedrick had already copped out to a deal in return for a stellar testimony.

When the attorney exited the room, I began to clear my head. There was only one thing left to do: memorize my story without faults so that it would sound more plausible on the stand than Hedrick's. Within thirty minutes, I was primed to withstand any type of questioning the D.A. was prepared to interrogate me with.

When the deputy came in to escort me to the stand, I was wearing a stone-faced expression, displaying no emotions whatsoever. The courtroom was at a dead silence. The judge shuffled around some papers that rustled like dry leaves skidding across a concrete walk. My stonewall barrier remained impregnable. After I was sworn in, I looked out into the sea of watchful malignancy. I had seen many trials on Court TV where the person on the stand bowed their heads limply as if they were already found guilty. I refused to give the spectators a cowardly display. Those same cold stares that beat against my shield, vigilantly trying to crack the surface, were returned right back to them. Some lowered their heads when I glanced at them, and others scowled back at me.

The district attorney, with his paunchy gut and loosely hanging jowls, approached the stand and asked me to state my full name for the court records. He then started to ask me his first question, pausing for emphasis with the jury. The first few were the normal blasé... blasé... about whether I knew the defendant, how long we were acquainted, what type of friendship we had. He then started going over the events that led up to the robbery, backtracking and restating questions to try and trip me up in a lie. I stuck to the same script that I had so vividly memorized in my mind, stating over and over that Dre had no involvement in the initial planning of the robbery. It was a must that the jury interpret the meaning I was trying to get across to them. As long as they understood that Dre had no knowledge of the robbery until we arrived at the store, then his chances of winning the case were going to be much greater.

I knew I was risking a perjury charge by altering the facts a bit, but I was willing to stick my neck on the line because there was a life at stake. Not just any life, but my homie that I knew personally.

Suddenly, the D.A. changed his strategy, raising and lowering his voice with every question to try and get me to show anger. Dre's lawyer, sensing what he was trying to do, began objecting to a line of questioning, but the judge overruled them, of course.

That impenetrable shield that I encased myself in was slowly being deteriorated by the D.A.'s tactics. I did not prepare myself for the intense line of questioning—just the surface stuff I imagined from my lack-of-lawyer-knowledge perspective. When my underarms began sweating profusely, I clapped my arms tightly by my sides so that the half-moons of perspiration would not betray my nervousness. I could feel myself slipping over the edge of the cliff, barely hanging on to that one root that was liable to snap at any moment, dropping me into that endless pit of destruction.

Just when my temper was about to surmount beyond a level of measurable control, I caught a glimpse of Dre's attorney shaking his head from side to side. Beside him, Dre had his hands cupped up under his chin in a sort of prayer motion—probably asking God to calm my eruption to save his life. It was at that moment that I realized what the D.A. was doing. He knew that if he could get me to show my violent side, then my thinking process would become irrational, which in turn would expose my vulnerabilities and contradictions in my testimony. That would make me an out-of-control witness with a motive, doing more damage to Dre's case.

Ignoring the D.A.'s question, I took fifteen seconds to regain my composure. This gave my temper time to settle from a raging boil to a meticulous standstill. A rosy pink flush stained the D.A.'s cheeks as he waited for me to respond. He began to repeat the question, a little louder this time, but I cut him off midway with an answer. It came out so calm and crisp that even I was shocked. The D.A. was flustered. He turned toward the jury and snapped, "This man is a trained liar. I have no further questions, Your Honor."

With that comment, he showed he was no longer in control, losing a substantial part of his grip on the case.

Dre's attorney, a balding, middle-aged Black man in a designer suit, stood up and approached the stand. He moved with a slow gait, giving the jury and spectators time to focus on him. Like the D.A. before him, he asked me to state my full name for the record, then started questioning me about the events leading up to the robbery. I stuck to the story like Gorilla Glue, staying consistent with the details while making Dre seem all the more innocent.

The D.A., sensing the case slipping through his fingers, began shouting rude outbursts in an attempt to shake Dre's lawyer.

"Your Honor, this is a cat and mouse game! Can't you see this cowboy is leading the witness? This is turning into a rodeo show where the cowboy's trying to rescue the untamed horse!"

Finally, Dre's attorney snapped.

"Your Honor, can you please tell this man to stop making rude comments while I'm cross-examining the witness?"

Before he could finish, the D.A. jumped to his feet.

"Oh please, let's cut the crap. The only thing I'm trying to do is present the court with actual facts, not some led-on testimony from a man who's already admitted guilt in the robbery."

Dre's lawyer fired back with something close to throwing a punch.

"Now you hold it right there—I'm not about to sit up here and take another one of your degrading comments. You're rude, and I'm not bowing down to you."

The judge, who had been watching the chaos unfold from over the rim of his glasses, had enough. He set his glasses on the podium, pinched the bridge of his nose, and started hollering.

"Wait just a minute here. I don't think you two know me very well, but it's about time you do. This circus you've brought into my courtroom ends now. The next person to interrupt will be held in contempt. Do you gentlemen fathom that?"

Both attorneys agreed and cooperated for the remainder of the interrogation. Thirty minutes before the lunch break, they wrapped up their questioning. I gave the jury a hard look before being escorted back to the witness room. The dull, sluggish looks they gave me when I first walked in were now replaced with a fresh liveliness—something that looked like it could be in Dre's favor.

Back in the witness room, the deputy told me not to get too comfortable—he'd be back in ten minutes to take me over to the county jail for lunch. Just before he closed the door, he leaned his head back in and said, "You did an excellent job on the stand."

I sat back in the chair and smiled to myself. If I could sway the deputy's opinion about Dre, maybe the jury had a change of heart too.

When I got back to the jail, Cory and three others wasted no time asking how the trial was going. I told them, with real enthusiasm, that Dre's chances were looking promising. One of the guys chimed in, "I sure as hell hope so, 'cause if these rednecks find him guilty, they gon' try their best to slaughter him."

"Try ain't the word," I said. "Shit, they gonna put the noose around his neck. It's a must my homie beat these mufuckas."

After lunch, I started thinking about how Hedrick was gonna perform on the stand. I hoped and prayed he'd stutter and stammer, make himself look untrustworthy to the jurors. I tried reading a book to distract myself, but my mind kept drifting back to the trial. I turned on the TV to help calm the nerves, but the thoughts came back. By three o'clock, I had a pounding headache and no painkillers to kill the throb.

The only cure I knew besides pills was sleep. I crashed until Cory woke me for dinner. The headache was gone, but so was my appetite. I forced down a handful of fries and one corn dog, gave the rest away. The guys knew how big my appetite usually was, so they could tell something was heavy on me. They told me to quit stressing—that it wasn't gonna solve a damn thing.

When the inmate runner came to get the trays, the same deputy who escorted me to court was with him. He wasn't supposed to share specifics of the trial, but since I was involved, he felt I deserved to know. One look at his hard-set face told me it wasn't good news.

He let me know Hedrick had dropped a deathblow on Dre's case—spilled everything. The planning, the guns, who did what. The D.A. had to cut him off so they could move on to closing arguments. The deputy said Hedrick was performing like he was trying to outdo Whitney Houston at the Oscars.

If thoughts could kill, I would've gladly watched Hedrick's heart slide down the drain of a bone grinder.

The deputy snapped me out of it and reminded me that Dre still had a shot. But I felt myself sinking back into that pool of hopelessness. I thanked him for the info, then went back to my cell to drown in guilt. All night, I thought about Dre's family—his mom, his pregnant girl—and how Hedrick probably destroyed any chance of them being together again.

My eyes didn't get heavy with sleep until deep into the morning. By then, I'd almost worried myself crazy. I slept through breakfast and would've slept longer if Cory hadn't shaken me awake.

They were calling me over the intercom to pack up—it was time to return to prison life: imitation food and unchecked violence. I gave the fellas a firm handshake, told them to keep their heads up. All of them were either awaiting trial, already pled guilty, or sentenced and waiting to be shipped off. One way or another, we were all staring down a long, treacherous road. I knew some of them weren't gonna make it back from the concrete jungle.

I made sure to walk tall and proud when I passed by the female inmates. They were horny and bored, and it made their day to see a prison dude. The thought of an urban warrior craving sex just like them stirred up fantasies—getting their backs blown out in spine-tingling, gut-wrenching orgasms over and over again. I walked slow because I knew the freakiest ones were behind those doors, click-flicking just to satisfy the throbbing in their panties.

After I signed the county release papers, I was handcuffed and ushered into the deputy cruiser for immediate transfer. I waited until we were out of the county limits before asking the deputy about Dre's outcome. His eyes darted to the rearview mirror, trying to gauge how I'd react to the news.

"I hate to be the bearer of bad news, Ray, that's why I didn't tell you anything. But since you asked, I might as well say it. The jury returned a guilty verdict this morning, and Dre didn't take it too well. We had to station a deputy at every exit to keep him from running."

He was dragging it out. I could hear all the theatrics later. "Let's skip the drama. How much time did he get?"

Anger surged through me, my head heating up to the point I feared I might burst a blood vessel.

"The judge gave him the ninety-nine-year max sentence because of the gun. He snapped in there, and to be honest, I can't blame him. That boy was strong as a bull. We could hardly hold him down to take him to the back. He was so violent, we had to put him in the drunk tank until he calmed down. I felt sorry for his family. His momma screamed like she saw him get gunned down."

"Why the hell did he get ninety-nine on his first offense? I've never heard of a sentence like this before. There has to be some law against this down here."

"The only thing I can tell you is he robbed the wrong people in the wrong county."

"Yeah," I said aloud, "he robbed a white man in a county run by the deep-seated southern Klan, who found a new way to destroy a race of people. Had it been a black man he robbed *and shot*, he would've gotten away with ten years, if that."

The deputy didn't respond. He knew I was speaking the truth. Whether he was one of them or not, he was in those back rooms, part of the circle when they secretly planned their vendettas. Staying silent and not blowing the whistle on this huge injustice was just as guilty as participating.

By the time we arrived at Draper, I knew everything that had happened at trial. When the deputy described how Dre flipped out after hearing his sentence, I became more angry at Dre than I was at Hedrick. I ran through all the reasons he could've been brave enough to take this case to trial, knowing damn well he didn't have a snowball's chance in hell of winning. None of the reasons mattered. Someone gave him bad advice, and it cost him dearly for fully trusting that person—or those people—with his future.

It took five officers to restrain him. To make it worse, his mom was raving, beating officers across the head with her purse. She was screaming, "Don't take my son away from me!" the whole time, swinging her purse like a boxer trying to make a comeback. The image stuck with me, and I realized how close I had come to being in the same situation. My mom was old Southern black. She would've vented her anger at the system in a much more violent way.

I asked myself, how much more fucked up could a one-sided criminal justice system be? It wasn't just like this in Hick County—it was the same across the entire system, designed to wage a structured attack against the poor. Sure, we didn't have to commit a crime, but every race committed the same types of crimes. The punishment and banishment handed down to people of color was nowhere near equal to what white folks faced. White crime was always looked at from a treatment perspective: *What's wrong? Is there a psychological breakdown happening? What kind of program can we put him in to fix this? Which therapeutic program would work best?* Meanwhile, black crime was scrutinized through a much more critical lens. We were instantly judged as monsters. How far did we bring our violence into affluent neighborhoods? Did we invade the white areas? And if so, throw the book at the "big bad black monsters" we need to protect our children from.

The time handed down for black-on-white crime versus black-on-black crime was enough of a message to keep crime confined to the black side of town. It was clearly understood: We'd get second, third, and fourth chances to get back out on the streets if we did as expected. But cross over and commit a crime against a white angel, and justice would be final the first time.

For the nigger-haters who issued their wrath through the legal system, it was a victory. For the black community, it was just another life lost to an unfair system and another child growing up fatherless. The chance of that child facing the same fate as the father was a recycled method perpetuated across the country for job security. The entire system would collapse if the root of the problem was ever fixed. We all know the tens of thousands of kids raised to get those fancy law degrees to uphold the "law" and tradition—they can't and won't let it be in vain. The system must continue to maintain control and superiority over a so-called savage race of people. This was the real-life *Underworld*—physically superior wolves versus the mentally and technologically superior vampires. The saga was straight out of the book of life. Animals and humans cohabitating, but constantly at war. As long as the old elite perpetuate this thought, we will wage this war to the bitter end. No politician, no matter how high they climb, can change that.

Chapter Fifteen

As I was being booked into the custody of the state, I began to consider my chances of crossing paths with Dre again. It was more likely than not I'd see him within the next two years because the penal system shuffled us around so much that we'd probably end up in the same penitentiary eventually. I wanted to see Hedrick more than Dre, to show him why backstabbers and snitches don't make it in the penitentiary. The chance of that happening was zero. I knew my name would be at the very top of his enemy list.

When the wrist-pinning bracelets were removed, I felt free again. To be able to move around the prison and engage in activities at will, instead of enduring the twenty-three-hour lockdown in county jail, felt almost like receiving my walking papers. The back-gate officer instructed me to stop by the shift office to confirm I was still assigned to the rehab dorm. After all, I'd only missed four days of class—one day over the allotted three. The shift officer made a phone call to Mrs. Adams' office to check my dorm assignment. Despite her raspy temper, I mumbled a quick prayer, hoping to stay in the rehab dorm. Completion of the Crime Bill program was crucial for any chance of parole.

When the secretary confirmed I was still assigned to the rehab dorm, I felt like luck was finally on my side. For Mrs. Adams to grant second chances was a rarity. After I unpacked, I caught up with Willie on the weight pile and relayed the events of the trial, from start to finish. The more we talked about Hedrick and his Oscar-worthy performance, the angrier I became. I was seething with rage toward this one individual. He had incited too much instant anger in me. He left us to die during the robbery, then returned as a snitch, playing devil's advocate. He was double-dipping in the negative, and I hated every fiber of his being for it. They say hatred is never good to harbor, but I couldn't pardon this coward. Where I came from, we stuck to a sworn code. He violated that for an eight-week drug program in prison and a return to freedom.

I released the pent-up tension on the weights, lifting thirty pounds more than my usual max. Willie thought it was because I was full from the good county jail food, but I knew the surge in strength was fueled by rage. By the time the yard closed, I was so worn out I fell into a deep sleep just ten minutes after getting out of the shower.

I was still sluggish the following morning when we were called to report to class. It took me a little longer than usual to get dressed, and the baggy pockets under my eyes reminded me of the sleepless nights. I was among the last stragglers to arrive at the multipurpose building. This made it impossible to avoid Mrs. Adams. She stopped me in the hallway and asked where I was going.

"I'm trying to get to class before eight gets here," I answered, with a puzzled expression. She gave me that eerie look and delivered the bad news in a way only she could.

"I double-checked your absences this morning. It seems you've missed a day too many."

The first question in my mind was, why was she double-checking? Was one of the house niggas reminding her of that extra day? I was sure that was the reason. I wasn't ready to give up on everything I'd been through to let it end like this. I came up with a few good reasons why I'd been held up in court. I expressed the need to get home to my kids and family, so I could bridge the gap and keep my boys from becoming a statistic. I even lied about having a deal with the judge to return in the allotted time frame, but the district attorney had held me up an extra day because I'd testified for my co-defendant. My plea seemed to be working. Instead of telling me to leave the building, she stood there, pondering her decision.

That eerie look in her eyes was replaced with a yielding consent, as if her heart was softening. I knew she was about to make an exception for me. But before she could answer, Mrs. Willingham, the building security officer for the day, approached from behind, throwing hateful and spiteful comments into the conversation. I didn't know she was behind me, so when she butted in, I turned to face her with the speed of a cobra striking a mongoose. The sight of her alone, combined with her slimy attitude and bitter man-bashing from her untreated past pain, always aroused anger in me. This prison was filled with scorned women in superior positions, and they went out of their way to inflict pain on us. We reminded them of the bad boys who left them high and dry for the next hottie.

Mrs. Willingham was short, with the ill-natured features of a bulldog. Her face was pockmarked with freckles and scars from pimples. She was the type of irritating person we all disliked—squeaky voice, always spitting out negative comments.

"You ain't gotta stand here wasting your time with this inmate. Rules is rules. You said he ain't in the program no more, so that's it. You don't need to explain or say another word to this inmate. Don't worry about bending the rules for him, or nobody else. When you give me the word, I'll toss their ass out the door and march them straight back to population."

I couldn't understand why the black officers—especially the female officers, who were mothers to young men like me, trying to right a wrong—were so quick to bash the black inmates. We were already victims of an unfair justice system. Why did they feel so brainwashed to carry out another race's justice, upholding this modern-day slavery? They were the new-age whipmasters, wielding their ink pens like skin-cracking whips, writing long reports of violence to ensure the parole board would hesitate to grant our release.

This fat fuck was playing with my freedom, practically boasting about stripping it away. Then she acted like she wanted to put her hands on me. I'd never struck a woman, but at that moment, I was angry and ready to buck against her and any backup she could call.

Mrs. Adams sensed what the walrus was trying to do, so she came up with another solution to calm the tension. She told me to come back when class was over to discuss whether or not I was still in the program. Instinctively, I knew that meant I was no longer in the program. To grant me any favor would open an investigation against her, and

I'm sure Mrs. Walrus would concoct a story to ensure she remained the victor over the inmate.

I told Mrs. Adams okay, then turned to leave the building. The walrus wanted to press her luck. She followed me out the door, huffing and breathing down my neck like a castrated bull, ready to charge the handler who'd taken his kingdom.

My chances of remaining in the program were thin as a roach leg, but I had to try anyway. I went back to Mrs. Adams' office to find out the results, whether good or bad. When I walked in, she got straight to the point. She told me she hadn't bent the rules in the past, and she wasn't making exceptions now. If I reapplied, she said, she'd put me back on the list for the next class—if there weren't too many court-assigned inmates requiring the program for their release. I accepted my loss and began planning my next move. Giving up wasn't an option. To give up meant accepting my sentence and becoming just another statistic. There was help somewhere in this violent *Underworld*, and I had to find that rare sympathetic worker who still believed in rehabilitation over the new standard model: lock them up, throw away the key, and dump it in the ocean.

When my next progress review rolled around, I planned to ask for a transfer to a program camp where help was almost guaranteed. Each prison had its specialties, and I was currently stationed at Camp Gladiator. My next mission was a camp program, and there was one located within a forty-minute drive of my hometown. That would not only benefit me, but my family as well, who drove hours every visitation day to see me.

The following week, my name appeared on the job board newsletter for a job change. Tomato picking season was just a couple of months away, and I knew the warden would fill all the farm squads to capacity for the grueling work. Quotas had to be met so he could receive his kickback bonus. It had to be substantial because they only paid the inmates seven to ten cents an hour. Think about that and honestly tell me the state doesn't profit from keeping the prisons full in exchange for cheap labor, kickbacks, bonuses, and incentives. We don't hear about those incentives, but I promise you they exist. Otherwise, this system wouldn't continue.

When I arrived at the job board that Friday morning, there was an extremely long line outside the office. The line quickly dwindled once they started assigning jobs. It only took a few seconds to determine who would be on the farm squads. Some men, who didn't receive outside money, were excited about slaving away all day for a twenty-two-dollar check at the end of the month. To them, it was an opportunity to liven up their lives—use the money for a trick, start a loan business, buy canteen items they'd been craving all year, or trade tobacco and coffee for drugs. I wasn't concerned about any of that. I wanted my freedom as soon as possible.

When I entered the office, the warden glanced at me with a hint of recognition and assigned me to a cell cleaner job. I was shocked but elated. The men still in line asked me what job I got, and I told them I was on farm squad seven. I didn't reveal my real assignment because everyone coming in behind me would have complained and argued about the job. That kind of complaining could lead to reassignment, just to satisfy older inmates who couldn't hack it on the farm squad.

The following Monday was the start of my new job. The officer in charge of the crew appointed me to the first shift floor cleaner position. My job was fairly easy—just keep the floors swept clean until the two o'clock shift ended. The only drawback was that first shift was when all the prison administrators were present, so we had to keep the place spotless in case they decided to do a walk-through. If it wasn't up to inspection standards, we'd face serious write-ups for failure to perform duties and insubordination. Second shift had it easier since no one really cared about the messiness, except for an officer who didn't tolerate filth. They would order a lockdown with no movement until the dorm was cleaned. Second shift cleaners knew which officers to impress and who to avoid.

Once my two o'clock shift ended, the rest of the day was mine. I could shoot basketball, lift weights, or go to the library, but none of that excited me anymore. Activities like these kept men content with prison and their current parole setups. I needed a program to get home to my family as quickly as possible. Institutional football, softball, and the weight team were definitely not the way to go. The grim truth no one talks about is that prison offers enough comfort for men with no vision to adapt to the Underworld violence so much that it becomes the norm. The less contact with the real world, the less they care about getting back to it. This false reality becomes something to die for. Coffee and cigarettes are the currency of this society, and without them, you're nothing if you still want to be involved in illegal activities. The man with the most coffee and cigarettes controls the hitmen, the sissies, the followers, tattoo artists, and the level of violence in the walls.

It sickened me to be part of this degraded system because I knew I wasn't in step with my vision for myself and my children. I seriously needed to get out. Watching them grow up in pictures was torture for a man trying to transition into a family-oriented one.

As the days dragged by, I started wondering if my prison sentence would ever end. Hopelessness tends to visit more often as the years wind down. The lonely nights spent stressing over the time I'd lost with my kids were making my sentence feel like a virtual realm of punishment. Sadness invaded me daily, and stress headaches plagued me nightly. I watched the men go about their days as if they were in Utopia. They seemed to be having the time of their lives—ex-jocks, disbanded soldiers, hustlers, and the criminally insane—all living off the past glory of their sports highlights, traveling the world as soldiers, or reliving their heydays of material gluttony as big-time hustlers. Those memories were enough to sustain them because, to them, it was eternal bragging rights. It was even more exalting if someone from their community showed up to validate the stories. That led to street cred, which, in turn, strengthened their ties to their Underworld organizations.

The institutional life was driving me insane. Something had to be done, or I was going to worry myself into a coma. Finally, after coping for months with the struggle to keep going, I saw my name on the newsletter for progressive review dates. All the happy thoughts I had in that moment were bottled up to help battle the gloomy emotions. Hopefully, the good would overpower the sadness.

I attended the progress review two weeks after seeing my name on the newsletter. The warden, my classification specialist, and the head psychiatrist were all present. The classification officer did most of the talking. She read out the specifics of my case and reviewed my prison record. Since I'd only been involved in one incident, she recommended to the warden that I keep up the good progress and remain at Draper. My words were caught in my throat, and for a moment, I became speechless. My classification specialist slid some papers in front of me to sign, and that's when I spoke for the first time since the meeting began. I requested to be transferred to another institution as soon as a spot became available. When asked why, I cited personal reasons, such as getting closer to my hometown so I could receive more visits from my family. I also told them I wanted to transfer to a non-smoking camp. There was only one, less than an hour's drive from my hometown. I didn't mention that it was a program camp, as I knew they would deny the transfer if they knew that.

My classification specialist said she had no reason to dispute my transfer, so she would put in the request to central records, as they had the final say. They agreed with my decision to transfer to the new institution I requested. I was placed on the transfer list, to leave whenever a bedding space became available. I didn't know how long

I'd have to wait, but I knew one thing—Ray Rivers was going to win at all costs. I wasn't going to succumb to prison pressures and end up a depressed wreck, full of psyche meds and on suicide watch every other month. My mentality was built to withstand stress. I was a leader, and leaders find ways to cope and rise above all forms of oppression.

I promised myself when the judge first sentenced me that I was going to beat the odds of another black man getting lost in the penal system for twenty years or more, forgetting all about raising their kids and keeping them from experiencing this hellish Underworld.

There's a lesson to be learned from every tragic experience. What we learn from it can be the deciding factor between surviving or falling victim. I've learned to stay strong in the face of adversity. The more we struggle, the greater our drive to succeed becomes. The problem with struggle is that once you're battling it, the problems never cease to let up. It's one setback after another.

Less than a month after receiving my transfer approval, I got another letter through legal mail from the Central Review Board. It was the letter I'd been dreading. I didn't want to receive this news until I completed a program so that my review would be viewed more favorably. My violent crime and the acts that followed painted me as a criminal monster. I needed something positive to overshadow my crime and speak volumes about my character and need to reform. I guess getting kicked out of the program had made its way to the review board.

It was my parole setup. I listened almost nightly to men weeping over their set-ups under the cover of darkness. I could tell by their wails and moans—devoid of prayer—that they had given up on going home. This one letter doomed men and their dreams in an instant. It sealed their full integration into prison life. Men with less time than me received fifteen-year setups on twenty-year sentences. Most of them had criminal histories and were repeat offenders. I was hoping, since this was my first bid, I wouldn't be judged so harshly. We all deserved a second chance.

I was the last inmate in line to sign for legal mail. I shoved the letter into my back pocket and slowly walked back to the dorm. I sat on my rack and stared at the letter. It felt like a two-ton weight in my hand, and I couldn't bear the burden of it. I dropped it in my locker box and didn't even tell my family that I received a setup. They'd been asking about it from the moment they learned that we would be given a notice of a parole date by the review board within our first three years of incarceration. I was afraid to open it for fear it would be too long of a wait, making it even harder for my family to continue this bid with me. We were the tightest family unit anyone could hope for, but I was afraid this damnation would break our bond of faith.

After dreading it for weeks, I finally summoned the courage to open the letter. It was dark, and I couldn't stand not knowing anymore. My family deserved to know. They were doing this time with me, regardless of the setup. I ripped open the top flap and pulled it out like a hot iron. I scanned through the contents and almost dropped the letter. I know my neighbors heard me gasp, like I was seeing a ghost. I read it again and again. This couldn't be real. It had to be a mistake. I mumbled the setup to myself before it became real to me. I picked up the phone and made the call. I didn't want to tell my mother. I would tell my sister and let her break it to the family. I couldn't bear to hear my mother cry, as if I'd been executed by a death squad.

My sister picked up the phone, the usual excitement in her voice. Even in this hellhole, I was a motivator to her. She wanted to know what words of encouragement I had for her this time.

"Twelve years, big sis." My voice cracked under the weight of reality sinking in.

"Boy, what are you talking about?" she asked, concern creeping into her voice.

"These muthafuckas say I ain't coming up for parole until I've done at least twelve years in prison." The rage in my voice was clear. I'm sure she expected me to act out, to lose my resolve, but I wasn't going to let that happen. This was grim news—the worst I'd ever had to deliver to my family. They were so used to me being the head of the household.

Had I been alone, I probably would have wept, but I can't recall ever crying because it didn't solve the problem. I was a solution-oriented person, but right now I was face to face with a mountain I didn't have the tools or strength to climb. This was a moment of facing life on life's terms. I had to accept it. There were no other options. It was time to plot my survival for the long road ahead. I had been swallowed by the beast, and now I was deep in the belly of the beast—the monstrous system that consumed men whole, digested them, and excreted them as shit to society. This was my journey, my reckoning with the choices I made that landed me here. It is my will to survive, but how? That was the question I didn't have an answer to.

Lord, bless me through this monumental ordeal. There is only darkness ahead, and I need all the light you can shine to be my beacon of hope amidst this Underworld and all the demons that exist.

Ray Rivers is a self-published author, motivational speaker, personal trainer, and business owner who has experienced and survived the urban trappings of poverty, gang violence, drug dealing, and prison.

His unprecedented story of how he survived multiple near-death experiences in the streets and in prison to the success he has attained today is a remarkable tale of triumph over countless tragedies. Ray's experience and leadership has led to countless lives transformed from the very communities that society often counts out.

His journey is fueled by the deaths of his childhood friends lost to street violence in hopes to enlighten the paths of more troubled youth looking for a positive example to uplift them from urban oppression.

Made in the USA
Columbia, SC
21 July 2025